Becoming Whole
In A Half-Assed World

A Primer to Lighten Up and
Balance Your Life

Barbara Reasoner

BookPartners, Inc.
Wilsonville, Oregon

Cover art by Richard Ferguson
Author's photo by Patrick Kenney

BookPartners, Inc.
P. O. Box 922
Wilsonville, Oregon 97070

Dedication

For Brad
whose indomitable presence — and spirit —
opened my eyes to the possibilities.

Acknowledgements

There are so many who help shape, influence and make a difference in how we look at and live our lives. For me, it was my parents who told me that I could accomplish anything; my sister, who taught me humor and supported me through the grueling work of building our marketing business and writing this book; my network of friends, who are there as sounding boards and strong shoulders; the many authors and their books that have opened my mind to new ways of thinking; and Ursula and Thorn, publishers, who march to the beat of a different drummer.

Table of Contents

Introduction

> If a person has had the sense of the Call
> — the feeling that there's an adventure for him —
> and if he doesn't follow that but remains (where) it's
> safe and secure ... he comes to that condition in late
> middle age (where) he's gotten to the top of the
> ladder and found that it's against the wrong wall.
> – Joseph Campbell

I think most of us are walking around at least one slice short of a loaf, particularly when it comes to living up to our potential. And living in a balanced way. In my case, I had bought into the "career is everything" mantra of the 1980s only to discover that, while proving I could hold my own in the corporate world, I had become my job. The person who was going to work, coming home, going to bed and doing it all over again the next day was me. And the half-assed world was of my own making.

Until that frightening realization, I was a self-help and personal growth virgin. I knew I needed to grow. I knew I needed diversity in my life, and I needed to try things I'd never before dared to do. I talked about it with my friends, and they felt the same way. "Next year," we'd say, "when things settle down a bit." One day it dawned on me that "next year" was 10 years ago. Things not only were not settling down, they were more frantic than ever.

> "No single event can awaken within us a stranger totally unknown to us. To live is to be slowly born."
> – Antoine de Saint-Exupery

I decided to take some action. And I finally had some time to do it after the birth of my son and an early retirement from my company. With a temporary respite from the daily eight-to-five grind, I decided to spread my wings and try new things. I took classes. I read a lot of books on a lot of subjects ranging from getting organized to quantum physics to various religious philosophies. My next step was to compile the most useful information out of all the books, synthesize it and devise a flexible plan for incorporating the best of it into my life to become a more balanced and whole person.

> "Growth is the only evidence of life."
> – John Henry Newman

I told friends, acquaintances and business associates what I was doing. Most jollied me along by telling me to write a book. "That'd be great!" they would say. They all felt out of balance, too. They were doing everything from taking steamer-trunk-sized briefcases on vacations, to checking their voice mail hourly on a weekend getaway, to feeling so guilty about doing something for themselves that any hope of enjoyment went down the tubes. (There's a fine line between being out of balance and being unbalanced!) Very few of them had the time or the inclination to do all the reading I had done. They suggested that a short and easily-digestible book would be just the ticket. That was the birth of *Becoming Whole in a Half-Assed World.* The title implies irreverence, not cynicism.

I discovered as I wrote this book that one has have to do some work if she is serious about her own personal growth. This is an active, not a passive proposition. But you wouldn't have bought, borrowed or stolen this book if you weren't at least a little interested in making some changes. You will start the hard work in the chapter on "Becoming Whole through Dreams, Values and Goals." Once you've identified these three things, the rest is a little easier.

I begin each chapter with a written value and conclude each chapter with an affirmation. The expressed values and affirmations are mine. You may want to change the wording to suit yourself. That's okay. Personal growth is not a one-size-fits-all proposition. Be sure to give yourself the time you need for this work. If you're interested in learning more about particular subjects, I've included a bibliography.

As I write about balance and lightening up and becoming whole, I realize how unbalanced, serious and downright half-assed I am — at least some of the time. I have to remind myself every day to maintain some type of balance in my life. I have to tell myself every day not to take things too seriously. I have to tell myself every day that becoming whole should be a

> "The purpose of learning is growth, and our minds, unlike our bodies, can continue growing as we continue to live."
> – Mortimer Adler

pleasant process, not something to "take on," like climbing Mt. Everest.

Some days I succeed. Some days I don't even come close.

Enjoy the process. The funny thing about becoming whole is that you'll probably never get there. What I've discovered is that the more I grow and change, the more I feel compelled to keep growing and changing. It's a never-ending process — and a whole lot of fun.

I thought you might enjoy some thoughts on change while you tackle the challenge of becoming whole, so I've picked observations by people whose thinking I like and scattered them throughout the book.

"Perhaps middle-age is, or should be, a period of shedding shells; the shell of ambition, the shell of material accumulations and possessions, the shell of the ego. Perhaps one can shed at this stage in life as one sheds in beach-living; one's pride, one's false ambitions, one's mask, one's armor. Was that armor not put on to protect one from the competitive world? If one ceases to compete, does one need it? Perhaps one can at last in middle age, if not earlier, be completely oneself. And what a liberation that would be."
– Anne Morrow Lindbergh

1

Who in the World Has Time to Become Whole?

In a half-assed world, you take care of everyone but yourself. To become whole, you give yourself permission to take the time you deserve for your own personal development.

⚜

Driving home in rush hour traffic, from a meeting that went two hours over schedule, my mind was on everything but the Spanish tape I was playing. My husband was in Europe on business (again), and I was playing Beat the Clock to pick up my son at day care. (No more Mr. Nice Guys at day care. Now it's $5.00 for each inhale if you're late.) Did I have anything in the house for dinner? I can't face rush hour at the grocery store, too. I'll eat oatmeal. Brad's easy — cereal with soy milk and some fruit. If everything goes well, I'll stick him in a stroller after dinner and get in my 30-minute power walk. Then bath for Brad, bed and a couple more hours on the computer to finish the marketing plan for my new client. Am I having fun yet?

My husband, Bill, and I were living the 1980s script of the up-and-coming dual career couple. Rising quickly up the corporate ladder,

> "Nothing is so common-place as to wish to be remark-able."
> – Oliver Wendell Holmes, Sr.

he worked 12-hour days and traveled. I put in long hours at the telephone company and racked up thousands of frequent flier miles overseeing television production work in New York and Los Angeles. I was accountable for an impressive, seven-figure budget for corporate and informational advertising programs. We took at least one big vacation every year. More travel and brief respites were our reward for working so hard. From the outside looking in (shoot, from the inside looking in), everything was copasetic.

The birth of our son, Bradley, was the catalyst for evaluating how I was living my life — and my first serious thoughts about having a balanced life. Six months into my maternity leave, I made the most gut-wrenching decision of my life and accepted a management buyout, making irrelevant the closets full of work clothes. Stripped of the job cocoon, I stood figuratively naked. Like a new paper doll, I now had to decide what my new wardrobe would look like. I would have fewer designer clothes, of that I was certain.

Facing change, big change, can be terrifying and immobilizing. I discovered as I faced the future that I had allowed myself for a long time to be pulled in a thousand different directions. Where's the time or energy for personal growth and becoming whole and balanced after putting in a day's work? Add grocery shopping, preparing meals (such as they may be), administering CPR to a relationship, doing the right thing for the kids, i.e. sports, scouts, music lessons, volunteering at school etc., house cleaning, laundry, keeping track of finances, myriad errands, remembering special occasions for relatives and in-laws, staying in touch with friends, making holidays special and taking care of our own personal needs — like a minimal personal hygiene program and sleep — and being unbalanced seems to be a normal state of being.

With all you're doing and all that you know you should be doing, it's easy to see why sometimes paralysis strikes and all you want to do is get into bed and pull the covers up over your head. That's how I felt when I started on the road to balance in my life. I realized, of course, that there are only 24 hours in a day. The good news is I could take the time to step back, evaluate what I was doing, set personal goals and start making changes in my life, if I was willing to give the project time and effort up front. I knew that I couldn't wait for that little wake-up call called a heart attack or cancer or a broken relationship as my sign to get started.

> "Death is not the greatest loss in life. The greatest loss is what dies inside us while we live."
>
> – Norman Cousins

Personal Growth Is Just That — Personal

I discovered that it is hard to measure personal growth. There's no paycheck involved in becoming a more spiritually-aware person. Few medals are handed out to people who have learned to set goals. There's a dearth of big buck product endorsements for setting and keeping a fitness schedule. You're unlikely to get raves at the dinner table when you've spent hours chopping fresh vegies for stir-fry, when all they wanted were fat-laden burgers and fries.

The growth you experience may not be obvious to anyone but you. Sure, if you decide that eating a little healthier and exercising are things you're going to incorporate into your plan and you drop three sizes, people will notice. If you decide to get sober and do it, your family and friends are bound to notice. That's the outside stuff — what I call the "show growth."

The inner growth (not to be confused with something malignant) is yours alone to savor or share with the special people in your life. Your inner growth is how you feel about yourself as thinner, healthier, sober. It's intangible. But it's more important, because it's not what others think of you, it's what you think of yourself. Easy to say, harder to do, but very possible to accomplish.

The first thing you have to do, as I discovered, is make the decision that it's okay, even necessary, to start giving more time to your personal needs and the things that will bring more joy into your daily life. This isn't being selfish.

> "We are wide-eyed in contemplating the possibility that life may exist elsewhere in the universe, but we wear blinders when contemplating the possibilities of life on earth."
> – Norman Cousins

It's all about self love. And it's absolutely essential if you don't want to end your life regretting what it wasn't. A by-product of being happy with yourself is that it can rub off on those closest to you and positively affect their attitudes and lives as well.

Make The Decision To Say "Yes"
To Your Life And Your Growth

Human nature being what it is, others will take advantage of you. It doesn't make those people bad; it's just that everyone can sense a giver. (Incidentally, one of the characteristics for people who get cancer is having a selfless, people-pleasing nature. I'll take being selfish — or having self love — any day!) Parents, spouses, children, friends, the committee you volunteer for, will leave you with no bodily fluids if you give the message that you're there for them to use at will. Is that what you want your life to be? A frenzied feeding ground for needy, life-sucking people?

I DON'T THINK SO.

A lot of people say "yes" to everyone but themselves. That indicates neediness — not by the recipient but the giver. It implies that you think so little of yourself you don't deserve to do anything for yourself. It also doesn't do much in promoting self-reliance or a positive role model for those who are leaning on and/or learning from you. Take a good, hard look and ask if you're a giver to the exclusion of taking care of yourself. If the scales tip that way, figure out why this is the way you operate your life.

Give your life the deathbed test. I did. If you found out today that you had one week to live, what would your regrets be? Would you mentally beat yourself up for not spending more time on your job, or regret that you hadn't spent enough time watching with wonder as a child (or a puppy, for that matter) discovered the world? One of my award-winning memories was watching my four-month-old son trying to grab a beam of sunlight shining on his quilt. Do you think you'd regret having spent a disproportionate time on the "shoulds" rather than the "wants"? Would you say that you really enjoyed your day-to-day life? Did you live your life for you? Were you waiting to start living when you reached retirement? Were you living for your children? Your job? Your next vacation 52 weeks from now?

Consider these following questions from *Your Perfect Right,* by Robert E. Alberti and Michael L. Emmons, to help determine the quality of your life. How recently have you:

- Participated in a new sport or game?
- Changed your views on an important (political, personal, professional) issue?
- Tried a new hobby or craft?
- Studied a new language or culture?
- Tasted a new food, smelled a new aroma, listened to a new song?
- Allowed yourself to cry, to say "I care about you" or to acknowledge that you were afraid?
- Watched the sun (or moon) rise or set, a bird soar on the currents or a flower open to the sun?
- Made a new friend or cultivated an old friendship?
- Stopped to "listen" to what was going on inside you?
- Spontaneously expressed a feeling — anger, joy, fear, sadness — without "thinking about it"?
- Done something that no one (including you) expected you to do?

- Done what felt right to you, against the advice of others?
- Allowed yourself to experiment creatively with new approaches to problems?
- Decided, by your actions, to direct your own life?
- Assumed a position of leadership in your profession, or an organization or your community?
- Risked sharing your personal feelings with another person?
- Admitted you were wrong?

You can have a more fulfilling, multi-dimensional life. You just need to figure out what it is you want to do and then make those things priorities — as big a priority as working and doing for everyone else. Yes, it will take more time and effort than sitting passively in front of the TV every night. It may even mean saying no to your children, friends or significant other and not getting involved in one more of their activities. Or paying someone else to clean your house so you can get your head out of the toilet and into a book or classroom or onto a jogging path.

This primer is about getting focused and determining what is really important to you, what you really want to be as you grow up and continue your journey. The following chapters deal with the different dimensions you can incorporate as part of your trek. You may want to add to or change those outlined in the book. I hope that *Becoming Whole*

> "Most people have a hard time showing up for their lives. Say yes to having a good life."
> — Neil Rosenthal

in a Half-Assed World will give you the cosmic goose you need to continue your life with a more balanced approach.

A circle is complete — with no beginning and no end. Is there ever, then, completion to becoming whole? Of course, the answer is no! But, ah, the journey, once you've started — as I discovered — is so exciting.

❦

I've talked to a lot of people about *Becoming Whole In A Half-Assed World,* and I discovered that many of us allow ourselves to be trapped by our "obligations." Here's how Susan, a 27-year-old teacher, described her prison:

"I feel really obligated to please others and to do the best job I can as a teacher. My job takes up all my time during the school year. Being this way makes it hard to do what I really love — my art. In terms of taking time for my physical health, it's the absolute last thing I do for myself. If I teach next year, that's going to be a focus for me because exercise is such a stress reliever. If I had the life I really wanted, I'd work for myself out of my house and would be doing something artistic. I think some of my moodiness stems from the fact that I'm so obsessed with pleasing people that I don't spend much time for just me. I've got to totally change some lifelong habits, like personalizing things so much, and I've got to try not to second guess things. I'm definitely going to have to change my priorities — like make exercise a priority, cut back on my work load and be satisfied with less than perfection. I don't even allow my teacher's aid to help me because I think I'm the only one who can do it. I set a lot of goals because I'm not satisfied where I am as a person."

A 63-year-old woman, Joan, told me it took getting a

divorce before she started to ask herself pertinent questions:

"I didn't even think about becoming whole until I was 58. That's when I was divorced after 33 years of marriage and raising four sons. A friend once asked me who was the most important person in my life and my answer was imme-diately, 'My husband.' When I divorced, a therapist asked me what I wanted to do with my life. You know, that was the first person who ever asked me that question. I've learned more about myself in the years since my divorce than I had in the first 58! As we get older, we all can take the time to become whole. It takes work and discipline, but you can start slowly and then build up. Ever hear the expression, 'Everyone is shoulding *all over me.'? I was a victim of that thinking. You have to be the most important person in your life and take care of yourself first and foremost."*

Affirmation: I value myself as a person and give myself permission to be the best I can be.

2

Becoming Whole through Dreams, Values and Goals

Value: I have dreams for my life.

In a half-assed world, you don't dream, much less have a plan for your life. You listen to the dream-stealers and settle for far less than you're capable of. To become whole, you dream your dreams and develop a road map for your life's journey, knowing from the start that there will be detours along the way; you may even end up at a far different destination than you first imagined.

I always dreamed of being famous someday. My first major dream was to be a Mouseketeer. Buck teeth, pigeon toes and a three-note singing range nipped that dream in the bud. But hey, with straightened teeth and toes, the sky was the limit. I wanted to play football, be a fighter pilot in the Air Force and then coach college football. Buy hey, I'm a girl in the 1960s, so no way. I made the decision to do well in school, have fun, make friends, go to college — and really have fun. Mission accomplished. Then I went to work for the telephone company. All my dreams and goals revolved around my career. One day I woke up and realized that my life was pretty one-dimensional, since the main topic my friends and I talked about was work. I needed new dreams and goals. I made them and my life was forever changed.

> "Where there is no vision, the people perish ..."
> – Proverbs, 29:18

Have you ever dared to dream dreams about the kind of life you'd really like to have? The "If I won the $50 million lottery, this is what I'd do" kind of dreams?

We dreamed as children, but as adults, most of us have forgotten how.

We seem to have let things get bass-ackwards. We've started paying homage to mediocrity instead of excellence. In fact, we feel we must somehow apologize if we make too much money (I'm talking in the ethical, old-fashioned, hardworking way), do too well academically (remember the tormented nerds from our school days?) or live an exemplary life in helping others in small, unheralded ways. Why be excellent in work only to have a big chunk of your paycheck taken by the government and flushed down a bureaucratic black hole? Why develop your brain when brawn is thought of more highly? Why get up and go to work when

> "Only mediocrity can be trusted to be always at its best."
> Max Beerbohm

handouts are available to those who won't? Somewhere along the line, a lot of our incentive for becoming the best we can be has been chiseled away.

Why Not Dream?
What Have You Got To Lose?

Most of us are just getting by, living from paycheck to paycheck. Worse yet, we've been programmed to be grateful just to have the job that's bleeding us dry. Or if we have a job that pays well with a certain amount of stability (does this creature exist?) and "status" connected to it, we've convinced ourselves that it's the best we can get; we'll never find the special job we'd actually love. Of course, if we're retired, we might think it's simply too late.

> "We are what and where we are because we have first imagined it."
> – Donald Curtis

We have to learn to dream again!

I know I spent a lot of my time letting life direct me. I didn't have dreams or goals. I just drifted with the flow. Flow is okay. Going with it is all right, too. But it's a good idea to be in the right river in the first place. Knowing your dreams and writing them down cements them into your mind so your activities are both consciously and subconsciously directed to do the things you need to live the life you'd really like to have.

Anyone who has worked in a corporate environment has undoubtedly spent a lot of time setting business goals for the corporation. And, if you're like me, you probably spent a lot more effort on the company's direction than you ever spent on your own.

Take heart! It's not too late. You're never too old to start dreaming and designing you own life. Eighty isn't too old and eleven isn't too young. The 80-year-old, however, may wish to make more short-term goals than the 11-year-old old. But you can't get started unless you start. That means putting your dreams on record.

Step 1: Write Down Your Dreams

Make a list of all the dreams you have for yourself. Don't think about the process, just go with your stream of consciousness. This may be difficult at first. You may stop yourself and say, "Well, I sure don't deserve to have that dream come true!" Or, "Did I use the right word here?" Push those thoughts aside and write down everything, no matter how ludicrous it may seem.

* Describe your dream environment in which to live — home, city.
* Describe your dream relationships with family and friends.
* Describe your dream means of livelihood.
* Describe the kind of dream world to live in.
* Describe the dream material possessions that bring you happiness.
* Describe your dream physical, mental and spiritual health.
* Describe your dream attitude about yourself and your life.

Write about a day in your dream life. Describe your bedroom, the sheets, the towels, what you see as you look out your window. What do you have for breakfast? Are you alone or with someone? Do you have children? A pet? What do you wear for the day? Do you go to work? Do you work at home? Are you retired? Keep going until you go to bed that night. What do you do before you go to bed? What are your last thoughts before drifting off?

Go through this exercise twice a year. Date the entries and keep them on file to compare from year to year.

Step 2: Write A General Statement About The Kind Of Person You Want To Be

I call this my Whole Life Statement. Whatever you want to call it, this statement will reflect your deepest values. You may be surprised by what you find out about yourself. It's worth the time it takes. Following is my own Whole Life Statement. You have my permission to incorporate some or all of it to help get yours written. I was in my early 40s when I wrote this. Had I written it at 24, I am certain it would have looked quite different. I suspect when I revise it at 85 there will be a couple of changes.

Whole Life Statement for Barbara Reasoner

My mission is to live a balanced life of integrity and to make a positive difference in the lives of others. I hold most dearly my family and friends, my mental and spiritual well-being, the quest for knowledge and careers that make me economically independent. I will be true to myself, and thus to others. I will never knowingly hurt another, and if I do, will always try to make amends. I have a written plan for my life that is flexible and changing — as I am. I believe there is a divine plan for my life and that in my own, small way I can make a significant difference in the world. I DO NOT HAVE TO BE PERFECT. I GIVE MYSELF PERMISSION TO MAKE MISTAKES.

Spiritual: *I "do unto others." I surround myself with positive people, pray, meditate and practice positive affirmations. My quest for knowledge includes those things that make me grow in my positive thinking and provide a deeper knowledge of my connection to God and everyone and everything in my life.*

Mental: *I'm not too proud to ask for help when I need it. I'm not too modest to admit joy and happiness when I'm in that state. Both are part of the human condition and should not be hidden.*

Family: *I treat my family with respect and am nonjudgmental of them. I allow them to follow their own paths through life. I ask for and expect to have love, respect, intimacy, trust, fun and laughter from life and my relationships with family members. I am available to my son to help guide him in his early years. He will grow to understand my values, but will not be expected to take them on as his own, and will know my view of the richness of life here and beyond.*

Friends: *Aside from my family, my friends are my most valued assets. I treat them with respect and am nonjudgmental of them. I help them when I can and ask for their help when I need it.*

Career: *My careers are successful. My sister and I have a financially thriving and harmonious working relationship in our marketing business with Nu Skin International. My writing comes to me easily. I am always open to new career possibilities. I am an accomplished and sought-after motivational speaker.*

Contributions: *As I fulfill my personal needs, I give back what I can to help others, with the knowledge that anything I give away will be returned to me in even greater quantities.*

Financial: I am financially savvy and have a healthy, but not obsessive, concern and interest in my investments. I retain trustworthy financial advisors to do this work for me.

Physical: I exercise three to four times a week, eat predominately low-fat, nutritious foods and take vitamin and mineral supplements.

Fun: In all the things I do, my goal is to learn and have fun. I travel, I study, I raise a healthy son.

My Whole Life Statement follows no prescribed formula, nor need yours. Yours should fit you well and be as comfortable as a pair of your favorite sweats and sneakers. No control-top panty hose or ties here. Write it, try it on and see how it fits. Then look at it again and rewrite it until if feels right. Every time I look at mine, I make some minor tweaks and adjustments. Have fun with it. If it helps, write it like a story with you as the main character.

> "Nothing happens unless first a dream."
> – Carl Sandburg

Step 3: Determine What Your Values Are

The greatest single value in your life should be to have some imperishable values, for as Lionel Kendrick wrote,

"Values are the foundation of our character and of our confidence. A person who does not know what he stands for or what he should stand for, will never enjoy true happiness and success."

Values are what make us tick. They're behind the decisions we make and the actions we take. Anthony Robbins has a lot to say about values in his book, *Awaken the Giant Within:*

"If we want the deepest level of life fulfillment, we can achieve it only in one way; by deciding upon what we value most in life, what our highest values are, and then committing to live them every single day. Unfortunately, this action is far too rare in today's society. Too often, people have no clear idea of what's important to them. They waffle on any issue; the world is a mass of gray to them; they never take a stand for anything or anyone."

Values are those things that you deeply and passionately care about. You behave according to your values. The following story helps illustrate this point:

The mother of a two-year-old was asked if she would walk a narrow plank between two tall buildings for $10,000. "No." For $50,000 or even $1,000,000? "No," to both. Would she walk the same plank if her small daughter was being held over the edge of the building and was about to be dropped? Without a second's hesitation came a resounding "Yes!"

> "He who has a why to live can bear almost any how."
> – Nietzsche

It's important to have values so indelible, so important to you, that threat to them calls you to defend them.

That's why determination of your deep values requires that you take time to figure out what's important enough to make you walk the plank. In coming up with your personal list of values, consider the various facets of your life:

- Physical
- Financial
- Spiritual
- Career
- Family and friends
- Educational
- Contributions
- Fun

Under each of these headings, list those items which are important to you. For instance:

- Physical
  I am physically fit and healthy
- Financial
  I am financially solvent and secure
  I am financially responsible
- Career
  I have fulfilling and lucrative career(s)
  I conduct my business with integrity
- Family and friends
  I love my family
  I love my friends
- I contribute to the world
  I mentor/help others
  I find a cause and help
- Fun
  I travel throughout the world
  I have the finer things in life

Here's a more comprehensive list of values I found helpful from the *Franklin Quest Success Through Personal Productivity Owner's Guide.*

I am innovative	I am honest
I am productive	I am teachable/humble
I seek excellence	I encourage justice
I am competent	I am organized
I have a positive attitude	I seek truth
I serve others	I am a leader
I am frugal	I am financially secure
I am physically healthy	I love my family
I love God	I am self-sufficient
I grow intellectually	I have integrity
I am generous	

Remember, these are plank-walking attributes for you — and just for you. If you wouldn't walk the plank for "I am a leader," then don't include it. If a value is missing, add your own.

Step 4: Write Down Your Goals, Keeping In Mind The Integrity Of Your Dreams, Whole Life Statement And Values

Just writing down your dreams, values and goals will, in some dimension, start making them happen for you. I am constantly amazed when I look back at my Whole Life Statement and my more specific goals to see how much I've internalized those into my life and more importantly, how much of what I envisioned for myself has actually happened to me. Having written them down and knowing that I fully intend to make them happen has set me on a conscious and subconscious path to achieving them.

In *Real Magic,* Wayne Dyer states that none of our goals can become reality unless we have intentions. I remember as a child I once prayed for a five dollar bill to float down from heaven and land in my hand so I could buy an outfit for my Barbie Doll. Sitting under the cottonwood tree waiting for it to happen proved disappointing. Once I offered my services for hire, my intentions got me to the five dollar bill (and I learned how to clean toilets).

As Dyer puts it:

> "Rather than simply laying out goals or wishes for how you want your life to go, try shifting to the active language of intention. Make a sharp distinction between what constitutes for you mere wishing and hoping, and what you are now in the process of intending to make happen. When I intend to be healthier, and I know this is the case in my mind, I usually get right up and do some exercise, even if it means simply walking around the block. The intention can literally put the thought into action."

"Most people's goals are as routine as to 'pay their lousy bills,' to get by, to survive, to make it through the day, in short, they are caught up in the trap of making a living rather than designing a life. Setting goals is the first step in turning the invisible into the visible — the foundation for all success in life. You can chisel your own existence by the thoughts you consistently project every moment of your life."

— Tony Robbins

Goals Are the Engines That Drive Your Values

Your goals need to be time-bound and measurable and in total support of your values. "I want to have a lot of money" is not a goal. "I want to have $XXX saved for my son's college education by 2014" is both time-bound and measurable. Robbing a bank to get the money may not support your values. Working at something you love doing and making a good income might be something you'd have an easier time living with.

Here's an example:

Value: I am physically fit and healthy.

Goal: By the end of this year, my total body fat will be 18 percent.

Activities: I do aerobic exercise three to four times a week. I weight-train twice a week. I keep my fat intake to 20 percent. I cook two low-fat meals each week.

Remember, in your lifetime (even in a month), your goals are going to change. Look at your goals as your living, flexible life plan. You don't have to ask anyone permission to change your personal goals. And they don't have to be perfect! Write them from your heart. If they don't look like the ones in this book or in your business, who cares? Have fun with it. Write what you really want — not what you think you should want. No one is going to grade you on your efforts. Review your goals once a month and modify them as needed.

Remember, it's the journey to reach your goals that's rewarding.

> "Being in the present allows us to experience the journey and to respond to the process of the journey. When we operate this way, we see that all goals are just temporary ideas that change as we draw near to them."
> – Dec. 13, 1992 *Women Who do Too Much* calendar

The importance of setting goals was demonstrated by several people I talked to. Here's what Cass, a 26-year-old, said about the value of goal-setting:

"Until a couple of years ago I had never taken the time to sit down and see where I really wanted to go with my life. For two days I pretty much locked myself in a room, didn't answer the phone and took a hard look at what was really important to me. Those two days changed my life. I am so clear now about my career — no, make that my life. I used to think I wanted to go the top of my company. I realize now that's not what I ever wanted. I feel so relieved to be free of that burden."

Lack of concrete goals can, as I stated earlier, set you on a drifting course. Here's what Kay, a 46-year-old mother, had to say in this respect:

"As a child I dreamed. I'd watch TV and see myself in a nurturing, glamorous family. I wanted to be like Harriet Nelson or Beaver's mother. Looking back, I was inane to fall into that role in my marriage. I got what I asked for. After my divorce I didn't feel like I deserved to have dreams. My first stage of being single was being in a survival mode. Now, I'm finally asking myself what do I want, what do I get to have for me now? I find that some people forget their

dreams or put them aside because of the day-to-day things that get in the way. I guess my dream would be to find inner peace and a sense of satisfaction of what my purpose is. I find that the reading I'm doing is allowing me to dream again."

⚜

In his *Six Pillars of Self Esteem,* Nathaniel Brandon places the responsibility for goal-making precisely where it should be: the individual.

> "I am responsible for the achievement of my desires. No one owes me the fulfillment of my wishes. I do not hold a mortgage on anyone else's life or energy, and no one holds a mortgage on mine. If I have desires, it is up to me to discover how to satisfy them. I need to take responsibility for developing and implementing an action plan. If my goals require the participation of other people, I must be responsible for knowing what they require of me if they are to cooperate and for providing whatever is my rational obligation to provide...."

James Allen anticipated Brandon's observation when he wrote:

> "You will become as great as your dominant aspiration.... If you cherish a vision, a lofty ideal in your heart, you will realize it."

In *Strangers Among Us,* Ruth Montgomery added her wisdom on the value of goal setting and how it works to create a positive emphasis in our lives.

"First, look toward your immediate goal and know that you will reach it. When it is time to choose between one direction or another, simply pause for a moment, blank your mind and listen to your intuition. Don't try to reason with logic. Your own inner sense will tell you which choice to make. If it is any more meaningful, ask for guidance from whatever source is most comfortable for you, whether divine inspiration, prayer or help from discarnates. Try being in the Flow as often as you think of it. As you test for yourself, you will find that it works. Decisions come more easily and goals are more readily reached. When you place yourself in the direction that feels the most harmonious, then you will be carried along to the accomplishment of each succeeding goal with greater ease.

"A strongly visualized goal becomes a spiritual magnet to which the necessary tools are drawn if one remains in the Flow."

In order for your dreams to come true, you have to take action on them. Following are the goals I made to accomplish the hard work prescribed in this chapter.

Goals:
- By (date) I will have written my Whole Life Statement.
- By (date) I will have identified my values.
- By (date) I will have written my goals.

Affirmation: I am in charge of my own destiny. I take responsibility for every aspect of my life.

3

Becoming Whole Through Spiritual Development

Value: I am spiritually healthy and aware.

In a half-assed world, you only value what you can see. You don't believe there is a connection between the spirit and body. To become whole, you must begin to place value on and trust those things you don't necessarily see or which seem unbelievable. You assign as much importance to your inner self as you do the outer.

❦

My childhood was filled with the invisible and improbable, starting with two intangible playmates named Honey and Sweetie Pie. My sister, I'm told, sat on them once, and I screamed bloody murder. I frequently heard my name whispered when I was about to get into trouble. Those whispers, conscience or Guardian Angels, kept me out of some pretty sticky situations, especially as a teenager in

Berkeley in the 1960s. My favorite "improbable" occurred when I was about eight. I woke early one morning at our cabin in California's Sequoia National Forest. My sister and parents were still asleep. I opened the curtains slightly and saw an incredible sight in the oak tree standing 20 feet away. It was an entire village of elves working away in the tree. I watched them for about half an hour until my father got up to stoke the wood stove and start the coffee. When I blinked, they were gone, and they never came back. I didn't tell anyone about the elves or the whispers because I didn't want adult logic to ruin it for me.

I don't think back about the elves in the oak tree too often, but I know deep inside me that what we physically see of each other is only the tip of the proverbial iceberg. A huge part of who we are is not seen. Everyone, I believe, is a spiritual being. This chapter isn't about what I believe. Nor is it about what you should believe. It's to remind you of the part of yourself that is bigger and has far more potential than your physical body. It's a reminder that you may want to take the time to think about the spiritual part of yourself and how this aspect can help make you whole.

> "Why is it when we talk to God, we're praying — but when God talks to us, we're schizophrenic?"
>
> – Lily Tomlin

In the Life and Teaching of the Masters of the Far East, Volume 3, Baird T. Spalding wrote of the power of spirit available to everybody:

"Spirit is the primary, vibrating, originating power; and you may enter into spirit and use its power by the simple acceptance of knowing that it does exist; then let it come forth, and the whole of spirit is at your command. To you it becomes an ever-potent spring of perpetual and eternal life right within you. This does not take long years of study, nor need you go through training or hardships or deprivation. Know and accept that this vibration does exist. Then let it flow within you."

It's far easier to give time and attention to the things we can see, like our bodies, for instance, than the things we can't, like our spirits. We can become so mired in the day-to-day activities that we forget there's anything more than what we're doing and experiencing here and now. When was the last time you looked up at the stars and wondered about the possibilities out there? Are there other beings? Does God know your name? Do you have a Guardian Angel or a whole flock of them watching and helping you right now?

Our bodies have limits. Sure, we can tone them, stretch them, build them and feed them. But our bodies will only take us so far. They will take us to the store. They will carry us though a grueling

> "Physical strength can never permanently withstand the impact of spiritual force."
> – Franklin D. Roosevelt

tennis match. They will make love. They will also shut down.

Your spirit, however, is boundless and has an unlimited warranty.

Your spirit needs a workout just as your body does. If you exercise and nourish your spirit, it will serve you much better and take you much farther.

In *Living in the Light,* Shakti Gawain describes our spiritual relationship in an unforgettable manner:

"After we are born into the body, we forget who we really are and why we came here. We take on the 'survival' consciousness of the physical world and we get lost in the world of form. We forget our spirits, believing we are just our personalities. We lose touch with our true power and feel lost and helpless. Life becomes a tremendous struggle to find meaning and satisfaction.

"But the darkest hour is truly before the dawn. When we finally give up the struggle to find fulfillment 'out there,' we have nowhere to go but within."

It's up to you to come to know your spiritual dimension. For some this is through organized religion; for others it is through studying many different religious and spiritual philosophies. It could be through Bible study. It may be by getting into nature, taking a hike in the mountains or contemplating life in the desert. It may happen simply by becoming silent and listening. It may be all or none of the above.

You may consciously start your "spiritual exercise program" early in your life or not begin until you're more mature. Or the conscious exploration of your spirit may be something to which you never attend, or even feel is necessary. This aspect of your development is highly personal and should be custom-made for you.

What follows is how I mapped out my spiritual growth. I include some personal stories here, because I've always found it interesting to learn how others have evolved in their lives. Mine may help you, or you may consider me a heathen. When reading what follows, remember that I have described what works for me, for now. You may have a far different view of what constitutes your own spiritual development.

I Attend Organized Religious Services

For a variety of reasons as I was growing up, I never attended church with my family. In fact, my earliest recollection of the family being together at church was for my sister's wedding. (She and I were hastily baptized into the Episcopalian church so the ceremony could take place there.) I attended a variety of churches with different neighborhood children. One of the things that struck me was how one religious sect put down other religious sects. I would read church bulletins that said nasty things about Catholics (the Pope ruling the United States through President Kennedy is the most memorable one). Conversely, my Catholic playmates would tell me I was going to hell if I didn't immediately convert. And, of course, the Jews killed Jesus. No mention was ever made of the far Eastern religions. I suspect those millions upon millions of people were considered so far off-course as to not warrant the ink the Sunday bulletins were printed on.

I was perplexed. If the whole point was to become closer to God, why was there such a rift

> "God enters by a private door into every individual."
> – Ralph Waldo Emerson

between the rank and file religions? And why did one religion have to be right and everybody else wrong? Don't all rivers lead to the ocean?

It dawned on me one Sunday, as I was putting my quarter into the plate, that religion was a business! No wonder each put the other down. They needed the discretionary dollars to build a bigger church, provide more cushiony pew pads, display better-looking statues of church icons. I became, I'm afraid, cynical about the "business of religion" at a pretty young age.

It was about this time that I made another important discovery. Some of the adults I saw in church didn't practice what they professed to believe in after they left church. Some lied. Some hit their kids too often and too violently. Some weren't kind to each other or to anyone else. Some cheated. They weren't doing unto each other at all! Did you only have to follow the rules some of the time? Or did the act of attending church absolve all those little indiscretions during the week? I felt uncomfortable being in any church. I felt like a hypocrite. I decided to sleep in on Sundays.

My parents, who had been sleeping in and enjoying the Sunday newspaper and coffee for as long as I could remember, seemed to

> "Every good thought you think is contributing its share to the ultimate result of your life."
> – Grenville Kleiser

lead the kind of life I'd been hearing about in church. My dad was an eternal optimist and honest, even if he couldn't quote the correlating Bible verses. An executive in a large corporation, he was a man of his word and had a great deal of integrity. He told me, and I believed him, that I could do or be anything in the world that I wanted to be. No church sermon ever gave me that kind of confidence in myself. My mother believed in only saying good things about people. In fact, it was very hard to get her to gossip about anyone. When life gave her a lemon, she really did make lemonade.

My eyes were opened early on about what I didn't like about organized religion. I entered my adulthood believing in God but not giving spiritual matters much thought; in fact they made me uneasy and embarrassed. It wasn't until my recent spurt of personal growth that I started thinking about religion again. To bring these observations to a conclusion, I have found a church that makes me feel good about being there. Its philosophy is one of tolerance and acceptance of different beliefs. I attend when I can, and the experience always makes me feel uplifted and secure in the belief that the world does consist of open-minded, non-judgmental and tolerant people.

I Participate In A Spiritual Studies Group

To enlarge my frame of reference, I am involved in a discussion group to talk about books and explore different religious and spiritual philosophies. It's a small group of people who are open-minded, non-judgmental and have no hidden agendas. It's very important to be able to "try out" a new thought or idea without having someone attack it or you. Gather a group of like-minded people to share ideas in a nurturing, non-combative forum. This is an extremely energizing and positive learning experience for all involved.

I Take Time Each Day To Appreciate Family, Friends, Surroundings And Everything I Currently Have

Let your friends and family know you appreciate them. You don't have to call them every morning, but you can quickly acknowledge to yourself that you're grateful to have them in your life. If you have children, don't let a day go by in which they don't hear you say the words "I love you." Perform random acts of kindness for family, friends and strangers with no regard to receiving thanks.

Also take a moment to appreciate your surroundings. Your goal may be to live in a different neighborhood or better house, but until that happens, "love the one you're with."

I've been accused of being too Polly Anna-ish. That's okay.

I Pray And Meditate Daily
(A Great Excuse To Sit Down
And Take A Load Off)

I read somewhere that praying is talking to God and meditating is listening to God. (I've also heard that meditating invites the devil or evil spirits into your body. You're going to have to decide that one for yourself.)

I've discovered something about myself with this activity. I'm a better talker than a listener. I find that I can pray taking a shower, waking up in the morning, driving my car or even exercising. It's a much more difficult matter to set aside the time to sit down and really listen through meditation.

I have a very wise friend, Ann, who has meditated for many years. If she's any indication of the positive influence of meditation, we should all beat a path to her doorway for her help and guidance. This is what she has to say about meditating:

"There are as many reasons for meditating as there are meditators — stress relief, creativity, healing. That's what starts people. The byproducts of meditation offer a much more profound experience. When I had my first weekend training and was doing a group meditation, I felt bubbles coming up inside me for no apparent reason. Then it turned into complete contentment. Everything and everybody were perfect. I had no idea it was possible to be so completely at peace. In yoga, which is what I do, it's called the Inner Self, the real us, the source of all the joy we feel in life.

"Why don't we feel this all the time? We pursue this joy and contentment on the outside when it's really inside us. Meditation has sharpened my intellect, healed old psychological wounds and immensely increased my capacity to love."

Ann is a mainstream, busy person, but she takes the time to do something each day that helps lead her to peace, contentment, awareness and increased intellectual capacity. So what's not to love here? Why don't we all do it? Again, it's the time factor.

Here are a few more reasons to meditate:

- According to Prevention Magazine, meditation may help ease anxiety attacks.
- Meditation allows time to unwind and relieve stress at the end of a day. At the start of the day, it offers a calm way to begin it.
- Meditation lowers blood pressure, your heart rate and gets you into the restful alpha state in your mind.

• Meditation teaches you to take time out for yourself. Sit, relax and listen to your inner selves instead of all the noise on the outside.

So now that you've become convinced about the benefits of meditating, you have to take the time to do it. But how do you do that? Take a course? Buy a tape? Go to a mountain and sit on a bed of nails? Drop out? All are possibilities.

In the spirit of not-making-something-so-compli-cated-that-nothing-ever-gets-done, my initial suggestion is to just start doing it. There is no right or wrong way to meditate. (I know this is blasphemy to proponents of different schools of meditation.) Start with small periods of time. If you like it, add more time. Get up 20 minutes earlier each day and meditate. Also, it's a nice way to end the day before you go to sleep. (And it sure beats watching the late night news before you drift off!) If you have an office, close the door once a day and take twenty minutes for yourself. You'll find yourself energized and better able to take the stresses of the day.

In the words of Franz Kafka:

"You do not need to leave your room. Remain sitting at your table and listen. Do not even listen, simply wait. Do not even wait, be quiet, still and solitary. The world will freely offer itself to you to be unmasked, it has no choice, it will roll in ecstasy at your feet."

There are wonderful audio tapes of music you can play when you meditate. There are tapes that guide you through a meditation, which are helpful at first until you can do it on your own. Once you're past this stage, pass the beginning tape on to friends to get them started. Count backward from 50 to 0 to start the process. If you start thinking about your "To do" list, start over. It's not easy to become a blank screen because we have so many important things on our minds. Let the thoughts ebb and flow. If you find yourself thinking about the mundane, start counting over again. Or imagine yourself in a peaceful, restful space, maybe by a stream, swinging in a hammock.

Once you get into the habit of meditating, it's like eating and exercising; you get hooked and want more of it. You won't have flashes of brilliance every time you meditate; you may not even get off the grocery list sometimes. At the least, you will reduce some of your stress. At the most ... well, the sky's the limit.

I Say Affirmations Daily

The world has become way too negative. Bad news sells, and I'll admit I'm right in there watching for a glimpse of unedited gore when disaster strikes. I can't tune in to CNN fast enough! Dwelling on disasters and concentrating on the low end of the food chain when it comes to human behavior is surely not the way we need to spend our time, however.

I've always been "the glass is half-full" kind of person. It's a partly sunny, not a partly cloudy day. Having a positive outlook sets the tone for the kind of day and even the kind of life you're going to have. A positive person looks at a beautiful sunset and thinks, "Wow, am I glad I'm alive right now so I can see this." The negative thinker says, "You know why the sky's so orange, don't you? Pollution. And it's killing all of us!"

The negative thinker is probably right. But you've got to lighten up and enjoy the moment. Once the sun sets, you can go inside and write a letter to your state representative. You can walk instead of drive the next time you go to the grocery store. You can even pick up some litter along the way. This is the way to make a couple of positives out of a negative.

I choose not to be around negative people. They are energy- and life-draining. Don't get me wrong, I don't have my head buried up in those partly sunny skies.

> "Great men are they who see that spiritual is stronger than any material force, that thoughts rule the world."
> Ralph Waldo Emerson

I'm well aware of the problems out there. I just choose to approach them from the position of what I can do rather than what I can't do.

Keep a list of positive affirmations and quotations in your daily planner. Clip out cartoons or amusing articles and keep them in your planner. When you have a minute — such as when waiting for an appointment or when stuck in traffic — read them. Keep a set of affirmations written on index cards by your bed so you can say them to yourself before you fall asleep at night and first thing in the morning. Here are just a few of my affirmations.

- I am always in the right place at the right time.
- I am a success. I allow myself to feel successful.
- I focus on what I love and thus draw it to me.
- My dreams come true.
- My energy is focused and directed toward my goals.
- I deserve abundance.

- I expect only the best to happen and it does.
- I have a unique, special contribution to make.
- Everyone's success contributes to my success.
- I know my value. I honor my worth.
- I appreciate myself. I give thanks for my wonderful life.
- I value my time and energy.

There are many good books on affirmations. One of my favorites is a book written in the 1940s called *The Game of Life and How to Play It* by Florence Scovel Shinn. Her opening paragraph is worth reading:

"Most people consider life a battle, but it is not a battle, it is a game. It is a game, however, which cannot be played success-fully without the knowledge of spiritual law, and the Old and New Testaments give the rules of the game with wonderful clearness. Jesus Christ taught that it was the great game of Giving and Receiving. 'Whatsoever a man soweth that shall he also reap.' This means that whatever man sends out in word or deed, will return to him; what he gives, he will receive. If he gives hate, he will receive hate; if he gives love, he will receive love; if he gives criticism, he will receive criticism; if he lies, he will be lied to; if he cheats, he will be cheated."

Shinn explains how your words determine the kind of life you will live. She demonstrates how you can change your conditions by changing your words. "Any man who does not know the power of the word is behind the times."

The giving and receiving Shinn talks about can start and end each day as positive thoughts in the form of affirmations. Saying good things about yourself, your family and friends and the world in general is a wonderful way to do something positive. It certainly can't hurt, and if you take the time to look back after you've been doing affirmations over some months, you'll probably even notice the positive changes they've made.

࿇

Ruth Ann, a 43-year-old woman, told me why spirituality is important to her:

"When I was 6 years old my brother told me he was ready to die and was going to meet Jesus. The next day, when he left with my parents, I somehow knew I'd never see him again. They were in a car wreck on the way home and he died. After that, I spent a lot of time by myself. I'd talk to my animals and just knew that God was everywhere. Throughout my life I've known that what you can believe you can achieve. I do believe that everything in my life has a purpose, that people come into your life to teach you lessons. Life is really a journey for spiritual knowledge. Sometimes I feel an overwhelming love for mankind.... That's what I'm striving to feel like all the time."

Another woman, Katie, 25, told me that she found balance and centeredness spending time in nature.

"It is there that I find a peaceful mind away from worries and society's pressures. It's there I'm able to envision my dreams.... I'm sort of a visionary, I guess. There are purposeful dreams I get through meditation ... an ability to tap into a heightened awareness through exercise. I keep a journal and see where I've set goals, where I've

reached them and then I set new goals for the future.

"I wanted to work at the '92 Olympics. I pursued the idea, kept in touch and eventually got a job with the U. S. Olympic Committee. In college I said I wanted to be an amateur athlete ... a mogul skier. The Olympics influenced me to stay as an amateur. I identify with my higher self in times of solitude, whether I'm in the dessert or at the Arctic Circle. The energy I feel is definitely a mind, body, spirit connection."

🙟🙠

It is the mind, body, spirit connection that expresses the ultimate striving in each of us for perfection, whether we choose to call it God, or spiritual energy or the power of the universe.

I've listed no goals in this chapter since I'd be hard pressed to measure if I'm closer to God or X times more spiritual.

Affirmation: I take time each day to acknowledge, nurture and develop the spiritual part of myself.

4

Becoming Whole Through A Healthy Lifestyle

Value: I am physically fit and healthy.

In a half-assed world, you take your body and your health for granted. To become whole, you need to honor yourself by respecting and taking care of your (yes, this is corny) temple.

I became a vegetarian when I was two. That was not the thing to do in 1951. Pediatricians were frantically consulted. "Starve her," was one's advice. Give it a rest and she'll "come around" was another's. Fortunately, my parents decided to feed me what I'd eat. What I'd eat consisted of raw vegetables, egg nogs, milk, fruit and anything crispy or sweet. To everybody's dismay (and the surprise of several doctors predicting dire consequences), I had an incredible amount of energy, did well in school, participated in all sports (even football with the boys), and wasn't sickly. As a teenager and in my early 20s, I gave

> "A vegetarian is a person who won't eat anything that can have children."
>
> — David Brenner

meat a try to "fit in" with my friends. I didn't like it then, either, so I gave it up, making my little furry friends and me a lot happier.

꧁꧂

Ask a critically ill person in a hospital bed with tubes coming out of his orifices if he'd rather have a pile of money or his health restored, and I'd be willing to bet his response would be "My health, you fool!"

Few of us are health saints. I've given my body its share of abuse during my early years. I smoked. I drank a little too much wine every night after work to unwind. In my 20s I did little or no exercise. (In fact, some of my rude but perceptive friends, playing on my name, Barbara Sue, used to call me Barbara Supine.) Ironically, in the midst of all this debauchery, I became a student of nutrition. I knew what I was supposed to be doing. I was just a little lax on the follow through.

> "As long as men are liable to die and are desirous to live, a physician will be made fun of, but he will be well paid."
>
> — Jean de la Bruyère

As I see it, the health care system in the United States has been operating upside down. The big dollars and attention are going to disease management (as in, "Let's see how we'll 'manage' that five pound tumor on your lungs, Ms. Smith."). Some money is being expended on disease detection — mammograms, blood cholesterol testing, etc. (as in, "After eating butter, bacon and eggs every day for 50 years, isn't it great we have this little test to show you've got a cholesterol problem?"). Little attention has been given to disease prevention. In fact, until recently, people who took a holistic approach to their health were dismissed as granola heads from Berkeley or Boulder and treated patronizingly by their doctors.

I used to do more preventive maintenance on my car than on myself. I'd take my car in for regular oil changes, have the tires rotated and fill up the windshield wiper fluid. How many men willingly go in for a yearly physical so the doctor can kick their tires and check the fluid levels? How many women put off getting yearly pap smears and regularly-scheduled mammograms?

Remember when you were little and played hide and seek? Did you ever try hiding in a really obvious place (like behind an anorexic tree), close your eyes and hope you wouldn't be discovered? That's what a lot of us are doing with our health. We eat stupidly and do stupid things — like smoking, drinking, taking drugs, getting too stressed — and we don't exercise. These are our little temples, and we're playing Russian roulette with them!

We have to stop crossing our fingers and hoping we won't get caught and start taking a more active role in, and being more accountable for, our health. We have to stop putting the burden of our health care solely upon the shoulders of our doctors. The doctor's job is disease detection and disease management. Our job is to take the steps to try to prevent disease in our bodies in the first place, and to realize that nobody can feed, exercise or nurture them but us. One of the steps we can take is to develop a preventive health care plan for ourselves.

Following are a few simple things that we can do to become more healthy.

Have Regular Physical Examinations

Get a benchmark on where you are health-wise, and then compare your results from year to year. A physician can order the tests you need. Explain that you want to become more responsible for your health. (If this is a threatening concept to your doctor, better shop around for someone else.) Go into your appointment armed with a list of questions you want answered. Again, if this seems like too much of a burden to the doctor, find someone who will spend the time with you. Ask the doctor for her definition of prevention. You're the customer. You're the one who pays. If your doctor won't cooperate, find one who will. If your area has health fairs, take advantage of them for the free or low-cost tests.

> "The first wealth is health."
> – Emerson

Find out what your percentage of body fat is. Knowing what you weigh without knowing your fat content is just about as useless as knowing your cholesterol level without knowing what your HDL and LDL and triglyceride levels are. There are computerized programs available now which, some say, are as accurate as the total body submersion technique and much more accurate than the caliper method. This body fat number will tell you more about what kind of shape you're in than your scales will.

Eat Mostly Healthful Foods

You are in charge of the foods you place inside your mouth. If you are overweight, overly fat and out of shape, you know how you got that way. You can bet your saggy buttocks that fit and healthy people know exactly how they got into the shape they're in, too. The fact is, as one authoritative health-facts book reported, the diet of the average North American consists of up to 43 percent fat.

Eating healthfully doesn't mean sentencing yourself to a life of tofu and alfalfa sprouts and things as flavorful as your kitchen sponge. It does means knowing what the fatty foods are

> "To eat is human, to digest divine."
> – Charles T. Copeland

and eating them only occasionally. Who among us doesn't have a favorite fat food and need to indulge occasionally? (My personal favorite is Ruffles Light in bed with the dip du jour.) This isn't about denial — it's about being smarter to gain optimal health. Try adding one more fruit and one more vegetable each month to your diet. The next month add another.

How much fat you should have in your diet varies depending on who you're listening to. The National Heart Association says 30 percent calories from fat. Dean Ornish, noted heart guru, recommends a more Spartan 10 percent to 15 percent. I try to stay around 20 percent to 25 percent. You should have the help of your doctor to determine what a safe level is for you (I'm really not doctor bashing, but you may have to shop around for one who even knows that fat is a dietary problem). Obviously, if you have a history of heart disease, the numbers may need to be even lower. If you're healthy and you want to stay that way, a higher number may be okay for you. Following is an easy way to get a good idea what the fat content is in the food you buy or prepare (I've based this on 20 percent calories from fat):

Counting The Fat Is Where It's At

If you want to lose body fat, you need to drop your fat intake to no more than 20 percent of total calories. Here's a formula to count the fat calories in your recipes and packaged foods — and you won't even need an advanced math degree:

Take 10 percent of the total calories and double, e.g. 120 calories x .10 = 12 x 2 = 24.

Take the grams of fat and add a zero, e.g. 4 grams fat = 40.

If the grams of fat number is higher than the calories number, you don't want it in your life — or mouth, for that matter. If the grams of fat number is the same or less, open your mouth and insert food. One more example:

A recipe for spiced oatmeal contains 180 calories. 180 x .10 = 18 x 2 = 36.

It has 2 grams of fat = 20. Twenty is less than 36. Bon appetit!

Arrange your pantry or food cupboard with the low fat foods on one shelf (those which are 20 percent and lower) and the higher fat foods on their own shelves (one shelf for 30 percent, 40 percent and so on). You'll have a visual reminder of what shelf you should be grabbing from when you open the door. Try to replace one "fat" food every month with a lower fat food, e.g. pretzels for potato chips, 1 percent milk for whole or 2 percent milk, etc. Over time, you should find more and more space available on your "fat" shelves.

Again, check with your physician about the kinds of things you should be eating given your current state of health.

Take Quality Vitamin And Mineral Supplements

As hard as it is to believe, the medical profession is still *uncertain* as to the need for vitamin and mineral supplements. The story we've heard is, "If you're eating a balanced diet, you're wasting your money taking supplements and will just have expensive urine." The news flash is that 91 percent of us aren't eating balanced diets.

In *The New Supernutrition*, Richard A. Passwater, Ph.D. says:

> "A typical American is not even nourished to the 'adequate' level that the RDA committee strives for, let alone the optimal level. One way to be sure you are getting an adequate nutrient intake is to take vitamin and mineral supplements along with your meals — even if the meals consist of the proper portions of the four basic food groups.
>
> "Even if all the nutritionists agreed on what a balanced diet was, real people choose not to eat what they know they should. It is true that we are overfed and undernourished. We may be food-smart, but we eat dumb. We tend to be a lot of talk with little nutrition action."

The few people out there who are eating balanced diets probably aren't getting the kinds of nutrients they think they are from their foods. Why? Because crops are grown in soil that's nutritionally depleted. Fruits and vegetables are harvested prematurely so they never get the nutrients they were intended to have. Storing, shipping and processing destroys food's nutrients. See the problem?

According to Dr. Daniel T. Quigley, author of *The National Malnutrition,* "Everyone who eats processed sugar, white flour or canned food has some deficiency disease, the extent of the disease depending on the percentage of such deficient food in the diet."

In Earl Mindell's *Vitamin Bible,* he writes:

"Most of the foods we eat have been processed and depleted in nutrients. Take breads and cereals, for example. Practically all of them you find in today's supermarkets are high in nothing but carbohydrates. 'But they're enriched!' you say.... Enrichment means replacing nutrients in foods that once contained them because of heat, storage and so forth.... Unfortunately, standards of enrichment leave much to be desired nutritionally. For example, the standards of enrichment for white flour is to replace the twenty-two natural nutrients that are removed with three B vitamins, vitamin D, calcium and iron salts. Now really, for the staff of life, that seems a pretty flimsy stick."

Now the problem is figuring out, among the thousands of brands around, exactly which vitamin and mineral supplements to take. Your supplements should:

- be gel caps, so they dissolve;
- be processed so they're absorbed and used;
- contain high, safe doses of beta carotene, C, E and the minerals chromium and selenium.

I read a story about a man who was draining his septic tank and discovered hundreds of undissolved, hard vitamins on the bottom. Be careful. There's a lot of junk on the market. You get what you pay for and cheap in the case of vitamins isn't necessarily a bargain for you, health-wise.

Take Responsibility To Learn About Health And Wellness

This is an easy assignment. Practically every daily newspaper has a section on health. Entire magazines are devoted to health-related topics. Subscribe to a magazine like *Prevention.* I like this publication because of its format. It has short articles and emphasizes prevention. I occasionally go to the library to see what new publications are available, especially newsletters like the *Berkeley Wellness Letter.* Attend seminars on health. There also are hospitals offering seminars on a variety of health-related topics.

Devise An Exercise Program And Commit To It

A show of hands please. How many of you left your house this morning without brushing your teeth? Preposterous. That's exactly how you should think about exercise, that you wouldn't leave home without doing it.

> "The only reason I would take up jogging is so that I could hear heavy breathing again."
> – Erma Bombeck

America has become a nation of overweight, overly fat, out-of-shape blobs. In fact, 75 percent of us are overweight and overly fat. If you don't believe it, go to a shopping mall and take a look around you. Go to a grammar school and take a look at the children. Even our pets are out of shape! The bottom line is, quite simply, bigger bottoms. Get yourself hooked on exercise, and you'll be doing your body a favor whose reward will be a longer, more physically fit life. It's up to you!

John admits he's let himself go. Do you recognize some of your own behavior in his story?

John is a bright, dynamic man who looks like a heart attack waiting to happen. He doesn't even qualify as a weekend warrior, since his physical activities occur much less frequently. He knows what he's doing to himself, but seems unwilling to make any changes.

"Work has always come first. I'm right at heart attack age, and I'm probably 50 pounds overweight. But I still don't do anything about it. Do you want to know something really stupid? I took a seminar on eating right, what to eat, the importance of exercise — the whole nine yards — and when I took it I did all the right things and lost weight and felt pretty good about myself. Then I just stopped and here I am. It's ironic because my wife takes pretty good care of herself. If she gains a pound, she starts watching her diet and exercises even more. If I decided to lose the weight and start exercising again, I know I could. It's just that I've got too much work to do, and I don't have the time to do anything more. Pretty dumb, huh?"

A lot of the other dimensions discussed in this book can start happening as a result of having a better-toned, exercised and fit body. Until you start moving it, you probably won't understand what I'm about to say about the benefits. By engaging in regular exercise you:
- Release endorphins that make you feel good.
- Burn fat and build muscle.
- Raise your metabolism so you utilize your food more efficiently.
- Help prevent heart disease.
- Reduce stress.

The list could be several pages long. The point is that exercise helps the entire body — both physically and mentally.

Look how an exercise program has improved Mary Ann's outlook:

⚜

The late-in-life mother of a young child, Mary Ann wanted to exercise to look like a mother — not a grand-mother! She once regarded exercise just as a physical release and conditioning, but has come to understand that it affects her mentally as well.

"I was lucky to be born with thin genes, but when I turned 30 I realized I wasn't going to be able to slide by on my gene pool much longer. So I was one of those who blazed a trail into the first health clubs. I took all the aerobics classes and moved up from the back row to the first row — you know, to get a better look at my buns flexing in the mirror. I even made tapes of music I took with me on business trips out of town. I'm sure the person in the room below me appreciated that! Exercise helps me relieve stress.

Even now, if I miss a week, I can tell a difference in how I'm able to cope with the day-to-day things. I don't sleep as well, my outlook isn't as positive and my waist starts to expand. When I'm 80 and have blue hair, I'm sure I'll be out there doing my daily constitutional, carrying a golf club to fend off the dogs and rapists."

I'm sure you agree with Mary Ann that exercise is good for you. But how in the world do you fit it into your day-to-day schedule? The answer — it has to become a priority. It has to be a priority at or near the top of your list. I am so addicted to exercise (not fanatic, mind you) that, like Mary Ann, to miss a week, which I sometimes do, literally changes my mood (lack of endorphins?) and not in a positive direction. I have less energy and am not as mentally alert.

My exercise program involves increasing my flexibility (yoga), aerobic workouts (brisk walking) and strength building (either free weights or equipment at the health club). You don't have to have the outfit and the athletic club to begin an exercise program. It just takes a firm commitment and a plan. Here are some ideas to get you going:

- Get up half an hour earlier each morning and take a brisk 20-30 minute walk three to four times a week.
- Do you have a television and VCR? Buy exercise tapes. There are excellent tapes for aerobics, yoga, tai chi, etc.
- Take a brisk walk at lunch time. Wear headsets and learn a new language or listen to a book or great music.

- If you can afford it, join a club. The expenditure should make you committed to using it.
- Instead of a lunch meeting, how about a walking meeting, or on side-by-side exercise bikes (don't laugh, I know someone who does this).
- When you travel, check into hotels with workout facilities.
- Get exercise equipment for your home. Work out watching a program you watch anyway — like the news or Oprah. Stretch on the floor while watching a football game.
- Start a walking group in your neighborhood.
- Put an exercise bicycle or portable stair steps in your office.
- Start a move to get a health and wellness program in your company. Such a program could even reduce health premiums and be win-win for all concerned.
- Involve your entire family — ride bikes and take hikes.
- Hire a personal trainer.
- Buy free weights and do reps watching television or talking on the phone.
- Find a buddy in about the same shape you are and exercise together. Monitor your progress and make some friendly bets.

If you have a "Yes, but" for all of these, then just get off yours and figure out something for yourself. This goes for any person, any age. The benefits will be immeasurable. You'll feel better and look better. What a way to build self-esteem and put the joy of life back into your life. Just do it!

Here are some goals you might wish to adopt:
• Have a yearly physical exam.
  Schedule an exam by (date).
  Schedule a dental appointment by (date).
  Find out your percent of body fat by (date).
• Eat mostly healthful foods.
  Review your eating habits and determine where the fats are by (date).
  Arrange your pantry by percent of fat contained in the food by (date).
  Invest in a cookbook or two featuring low-fat recipes.
• Take vitamin and mineral supplements.
  Talk to someone knowledgeable and determine what supplements you need.
• Read a health-related magazine (book, article, etc.) every month.
• Establish a regular exercise program.

Affirmation: I nurture my body in healthy ways. I am a vital, energetic and healthy person.

5

Becoming Whole Through Fulfilling and Lucrative Work

Value: I have a fulfilling and lucrative career(s).

In a half-assed world, you spend your life working for a paycheck. To become whole, you find work that you love to do and for which you are handsomely rewarded.

❧

On vacation I met the owner of a small shop selling coffees, rolls and iced fruit-juice drinks. He had pictures of his two children on the cash register and was charismatic enough to sell you food and drink you neither wanted nor needed. He volunteered that he'd once been a marketing vice president for a medium-sized company. He'd done well and had the goodies to show for it — big home, big country club membership, big expensive car. Problem was he wasn't happy. He never saw his children and had an iffy relationship with his wife. In what he describes as a before-mid-life crisis, he chucked it all, moved his family and bought his little establishment. They now may have fewer goodies, but they are rich in ways he says he could never have imagined.

Most of us have to work for a great deal of our lives. A lot of us form our identities through what we do to earn that living. Ask this question: "If I weren't getting paid for what I'm doing, would I still be doing it?" Now sit down and think about your answer. Really think.

Marsha Sinetar writes in *Do What You Love, the Money Will Follow:*

> "Most of us think about our jobs or our careers as a means to fulfill responsibilities to families and creditors, to gain more material comforts, and to achieve status and recognition. But we pay a high price for this kind of thinking. A large percentage of America's working population does not enjoy the work they do! This is a profoundly tragic statistic considering that work consumes so much time in our lives. In a few brief decades, our working life adds up to be life itself."

The Good Ol' Work Days Are Long Gone

Time was a person stayed with one company for a career lifetime — from the cradle to the grave. Job jumping was a sign of weak character, a sign of instability. That was then.

Now, if someone looks at your resume and sees you've been with the same company your entire working life, you're not considered to have breadth and depth in your field and are definitely not seen as a risk-taker. This shift in perspective is, undoubtedly, a result of corporate downsizing and white collar layoffs.

> "People are always blaming their circumstances for what they are. I don't believe in circumstances. The people who get on in this world are the people who get up and look for the circumstances they want, and, if they can't find them, make them."
> – George Bernard Shaw

Companies have conveniently changed the rules to fit the new playing field, so having that varied and checkered past has turned into an asset belonging to someone with an entrepreneurial and pioneering temper.

In the *Age Wave,* Ken Dychtwald predicts that the baby boomers will have several careers because the world is changing too rapidly for a person to count on any one job for an entire career lifetime. And with our extended life expectancies, our retirement funds (and who is his right mind is counting on social security?) may not stretch far enough given inflation and more taxes on funds already taxed at least once (sort of the refried beans of economics). Dychtwald sees our lifeline changing from 1) school, 2) work, 3) retirement, and 4) death to 1) school, 2) work, 3) retirement, 4) school, 5) work, 6) school, 7) work, and 8) retirement. We'll retrain ourselves many times and re-enter the work force several times in different capacities and may literally die with our boots on.

From Lee, survivor of a near-fatal car accident in college, you get the sense that she knows where she's going with her life and realizes that career change is in her future.

"A career is more than a job. If you can think of what you're doing as a career instead of a job, then you must be doing something right. Teaching will probably be my career for the next ten years. I loved student teaching, and I loved going there every day. I know I'll be a good teacher. But I also love to travel, and I'd like to do something with traveling some day. It's so hard to get a job nowadays. As part of Generation X, I think we're getting skipped. We're going to be the most educated group of people because we keep going back to school since there aren't any jobs. If I hated what I was doing, I'd send out resumes, but I sure wouldn't give up the job I had. Yeah, I think I can do what I love and get paid well for it. For now, I just hope I can get a job teaching somewhere."

Corporate "Force Adjustments" Are A Fact Of Life

While the changes in the structure of corporations may make some of us feel uneasy about job security, it's probably a blessing in disguise. It's going to force us to spread our wings and try out new things that we wouldn't do otherwise.

I was a willing participant in the corporate downsizing (right-sizing, force imbalance adjustment, i.e., please leave and here's the door because we can't afford you or your high salary and perks any longer) of my company. I agonized over returning to work after the birth of my son. Just after extending my maternity leave from six months to a year, I received word that the company was offering its managers a golden handshake (as in, take the money and run). Then I agonized over giving up a 14-year career — to become what?

I realized that my entire identity was tied up in what I did. It grieves me to publicly admit it, but I discounted women who stayed home to raise a family as not really "doing anything" with their lives. (What in the world could they possibly *do* all day?) And the last thing I wanted was to be asked the "What do you do" question and admit to "just being a mother." In my mind I was going from the smartly dressed, frequent flier, corporate czarina to a duster-clad woman in pink sponge rollers whipping up Spam casseroles and crocheting toilet-roll covers to earn extra money. But I knew intuitively that the buyout offered to me was a gift I'd better not let slip through my fingers. I also knew intuitively that I could make it on my own.

I left my company, I survived, I thrived. And so can you, if you'll believe in yourself and give yourself the chance.

In *The Popcorn Report,* Faith Popcorn describes the exodus from the corporations as a major trend she calls Cashing Out. She says that in the Seventies we worked to live and in the Eighties we lived to work. Now, we simply want to live — long and well. Cashing Out has become the way to do it.

> "Traditional corporate success demands extraordinary, exhausting effort. We seem to be saying, 'Is this stress really worth the reward?' 'Isn't this life I'm living shortening my life?' And the favorite refrain of our time,

'Is this all there is?' Adding to that already powerful exit-motivator is our lack of trust in the benevolence of big institutions. We don't believe in the essential goodness of our government anymore. We have no faith in 'parental corporations,' and why should we? They've failed to deliver on the basic premise of the relationship: a promise of security in exchange for loyal nine-to-five-ism. We're being laid off as corporations are being bought and sold like Monopoly properties. Our health and other benefits are being cut back. Labor's classic mistrust of management has 'trickled up' to management itself. But instead of revolution, we are seeing retreat. Away from the cold, sterile, alienating office and back to the welcoming warmth of the cocoon: the home business, thanks to today's technology."

Some of us are lucky enough to hurl ourselves out of the nest with a, ahem, nest egg. But a lot are unceremoniously tossed out with no departing gifts. The survivors of the purge are given the unspoken message that they're-just-darn-lucky-to-have-a-job-in-this-dog-eat-dog-market and

"The return from your work must be the satisfaction which that work brings you and the world's need of that work. With this, life is heaven or as near heaven as you can get. Without this — with work which you despise, which bores you and which the world does not need — this life is hell."

— William Edward Burghardt Du Bois

begin doing the work of yeomen (yeopersons?). I look at my friends who are still there and see them working longer hours under intense pressure. Ask any of them if they'd be putting themselves though this if they weren't being paid, and you'd be laughed at.

Preparing For Your Next Career(s)

In the corporate womb, I was well taken care of financially. But there was a big price to be paid for the oxymoron known as corporate security. It's called "not having a life." I wasn't even aware of it until after I'd put some distance between my old life and my new one. Like a lot of things, it's something you have to experience for yourself. If anyone had tried to tell me during my Bataan-like death march up the corporate ladder that I'd write a book, have my own health and wellness marketing company, and do it all in non-designer sweats, I would have asked what drugs they were on.

> "If we all did the things we were capable of doing, we would literally astound ourselves."
> – Thomas A. Edison

So, short of robbing a bank or winning the lottery, what do you do if the present situation is no longer satisfying, has never been satisfying, you think you're about to be thrown out of the nest or you're already out the door? There are a lot of books on the subject, so I'll just give a short list of things to consider:

- Talk to everyone you know about their jobs and the companies they work for.
- Talk to the person who has the job you're really interested in. Have her tell you about the

good and the bad parts, so you can make a well-informed decision as to whether this is the kind of job you really want. When you see all the warts and wild hairs, you may change your mind.

• Go to companies you're interested in and conduct informational interviews.

• Buy magazines on industries that interest you and read them. You'd be surprised how many jobs you could find for yourself inside that industry.

• Providing you want to stay with your company, look for a job inside. Make contacts, schmooz. It's easier to find a new job while you still have one.

• If your company offers you a golden handshake (fewer are doing so these days) and out-placement services, take advantage of all the free goodies they have to offer.

• Take advantage of your company tuition-aid plan and get trained for something you'd really like to do.

• Take tests to find what your interests are, or go with something you feel passionate about.

• Always keep updated resumes with you to give to people.

• Call every reputable headhunter you've heard about and interview them.

• If you're not currently working, sign up with a temp agency. This a great way to look over a company.

• Sell yourself back to your old company as a free-lancer or contract worker.

- Start a side-line business as an insurance policy — the extra effort expended now could set you up in the event of company "right sizing."
- Become involved in local and/or national politics.

You need to approach your career the way you need to approach your health — proactively. Wake up to the fact that no one else is going to take care of you. Most governments are in big trouble financially because of this philosophy. You, and you alone, are in control of your career. If you work for anybody other than yourself, you should have a backup plan. Open yourself up to the possibilities.

If you're not happy with what you're doing, determine what will make you happy — not what makes your parents happy or your significant other happy or your first grade teacher happy. Hopefully, there are a lot of things that make you happy. Sit down and figure out which of those things you might be able to parlay into a money-making venture. For instance, I love to do needlework, and if I could sell my quilt for $100,000, I'd have a lucrative new business venture, but I'm not banking on it. I do bank on my skills as a writer, speaker, organizer and entrepreneur.

What I am banking on, over the long haul, is my career with the network marketing company, Nu Skin International, Inc., and its health care division, Interior Design Nutritionals. The appeal of this multilevel marketing company is that I can work my own hours from home and work with people I like (unlike having to put up with a boss, peers and subordinates that you may not like). The other appeal is that my success is directly determined by how I can help make those I've brought into the business with me successful. Network marketing is the antithesis to conventional business where, if your subordinate does too well, he or she may take your job.

This particular career move has not been unanimously accepted by my friends and family. I've chosen to stay with it because it fulfills something that was

> "The average person will tell you almost anything can't be done."
> – Florence Scovill Shinn

missing in my former working life. I genuinely like helping people look and feel better with the products I market, plus I've been able to introduce people to the concept of being able to start their own business with no financial risk attached to it. Faith Popcorn says, "Nobody works harder or happier or more productively, than people working for themselves."

In *Do What you Love, the Money will Follow,* Marsha Sinetar observed:

> "The third aspect of 'the money will follow' is the ability to think well of ourselves and our capabilities even without money.... It is important to acknowledge that each person who embarks on a new vocational path may be subject to strong negative self-opinions if money is not forthcoming quickly or in ample supply. This is certainly true in America where we typically equate success and money. The successful person in our society is the one who has a great deal of money. The unsuccessful person is the one who is poor. Our own self-evaluation — our subjective comfort and discomfort — is critical during the early

stages of waiting for our financial security.

"The person who chooses to work at something which society doesn't value, or who works at a job which his friends and family say is not worthwhile, must transcend whatever biases others put in his way and stay with the job anyway."

Find some thing or some things you love doing. Then stick with them! Don't let the naysayers get you down or steal your dreams. Put on blinders and go with what feels right for you. I have learned more about

> "Wealth is not in making money, but in making the man while he is making money."
> – John Wicker

what I'm made of after leaving my "real" job than I would have ever given myself credit for. I sell, I teach, I learn, I nurture, I write, I fearlessly, but wisely, try new ventures. I love what I do — the money follows. What a trip!

What's The Worst That Can Happen If You Follow Your Dream And Separate From The Herd?

- You might get shot down for trying to realize your dreams by those you leave behind.
- You might get told all of the ways you will fail.
- Worse yet, your new pursuit(s) might be ignored.
- Your family and friends could try to invalidate what you're doing by playing deaf and dumb and stupid!

- You might get a guilt trip from remarks that you're ignoring your family and friends.
- You might get told that if you don't stop following your dreams, so and so won't love you any more.
- You might kick yourself in the behind if you let whatever anyone else thinks of you and your endeavors slow you down, or worse, stop you in your tracks.

❧

Talk about a positive attitude, read Jill's comments on this subject:

At 39, she could be the mother in the 1990s version of the Donna Reed Show. Her daughter looks like her, her son is a spitting image of Dad. She and her husband were on the cover of an early 1990s edition of *Fortune* magazine featuring them as a "green," earth-friendly family. Jill is always busy, always involved. This kind of busy would drive most of us over the edge. Not Jill.

"I've always loved what I'm doing. I've quit very lucrative jobs to go do something that I like. When I have found myself not totally fulfilled by my work, I've compensated for it by going to graduate school, getting my broker's license and teaching business classes. In fact, I may be over-stimulated at times! When I see what I'm missing through my work, I try to find it somewhere else. I feel there's another important aspect in having a fulfilling career — and that's always doing my best. I've seen people who are getting ready to retire sort of checking out. I always want to finish well. I feel that if you work at something that makes you happy, you'll make others happy. I know this

isn't supposed to be religious, but for me, personally, I think God is involved, too. I've always known that I'll do okay. Because I believe there's someone else, I've never worried about money or my job."

What's the best that can happen to you by following your dreams?

- You might find out what you've been missing in your life by "playing it safe."
- You might find worlds open up for you that you'd never even thought about!
- You might find that you're more creative and energetic than you ever thought possible.
- You might attract a whole new group of friends who, like you, are willing to stick their necks out to try something new. There's a whole different energy in being around risk-takers and people who love what they do.
- You might find that it no longer matters what others think of you — and you'll have a lot more freedom because of it.
- You might find yourself sadly saying goodbye to some of the people in your life who can't relate to the path you're on and don't understand you anymore.
- You might find yourself with an indelible grin on your face.

In order to be proactive about your career, it's a good idea to establish some goals, such as:

- By (date) I will take an inventory of my skills and interests.
- By (date) I will network regularly and benefit from the experience of others.
- By (date) I will have a backup plan for my present job.

Affirmation: I do work that I love and get paid extremely well for it.

6

Becoming Whole through Financial Security

Value: I am financially responsible.

In a half-assed world you're always concerned about money. To become whole, you must have a financial plan for your life. This frees you to work on the fun and meaningful things in life.

A friend from college recently filed for bankruptcy. She and her husband had maxed out six credit cards and were up to their necks in debt. Both had good jobs, but they had been living far beyond their means. And, now in their late forties, they have no retirement fund. She figures they'll have to work until they die. In a small voice, she says she hopes she doesn't live all that long with this as her future.

The subject of money is an emotional and volatile topic. It's one a lot of people dance around rather than confront directly. How you deal with money is largely a reflection of how the people closest to you viewed it (your parents, for instance), and the importance they placed on it in their lives, how they reacted to having it or not having it, by whom and in what spirit it was controlled. If money was a BIG DEAL to them, for better or worse, it will be a BIG DEAL to you, too, although you may not do things in exactly the same way they did.

In *Living in the Light,* Shakti Gawain writes:

"If you have too little money, you're always struggling to get more money and always afraid there won't be enough. There's always that terrible pain that you don't have enough of what you need. On the other hand, if you have a lot of money, it's painful because you're always afraid you're going to lose it. You can never have enough money to ensure that you won't be afraid."

Putting money in the correct perspective by making it part of the equation, not the answer to the equation, is easier said than done. Money should be the means to

> "Money, it turned out, was exactly like sex, you thought of nothing else if you didn't have it and thought of other things if you did."
> – James Baldwin

an end. But, unfortunately, if you don't have it, money tends to become the end toward which you expend all of your energy. The ideal is to get to a place where you know that you'll have the money you need (preferably a lot more) to make your life comfortable (preferably very comfortable) without thinking about it and worrying about it all the time (preferably never). Some of this is going to require the right frame of mind (faith); some of it will require the right goals (intent). I'll address the last first.

Save Money Every Month

Pay yourself first. The rule of thumb should be 10 percent of what you make. As your income increases, pay yourself even more. Even if you only sock away a small amount each month, at least it's a start. When you're in your twenties, it seems like you have an eternity to start saving later. One day you wake up and find yourself in your mid-40s with no retirement fund started and only 15 years to do something about it! It's not too late, no matter what your age. Start now. If you work for a company, don't fail to take advantage of its savings plan. It's a no-brainer way to save money. Money you never see is easier to save. If you're self-employed, set up a SEP/IRA.

Pay All Your Bills Every Month

The ideal situation is to have no debt. In these times, that ideal is not likely. In the best of circumstances, most of us will at least have rent or a house payment to make. But that doesn't have to stop you from coming up with a plan with this ideal in mind. If you've piled up debt on a number of credit cards, consolidate and pay them off before charging again. This is going to take self-discipline and require a delay in your tendency toward instant gratification. Ask people who've been in debt and paid it off about how much control more they felt they had in their lives. There are free financial services available in most cities to help come up with a payment plan. Otherwise, just suck it in and begin paying. Tear up your cards so you won't be tempted to charge if you fall off the wagon.

As a vice president at A.G. Edwards, Lola is a light in the soulless world of stocks, bonds and mutual funds. She's a pixie whose clients know they're never being hustled. She says:

> "If I were advising my own children or any new client, I'd tell them to use credit cards sparingly and to pay off their credit card debts as soon as possible. Paying interest on credit cards every month is a bad use of your money. I'd also tell them to start saving money every single month, even if it's only $50 a month. All the really financially successful middle-aged clients started saving at a young age with jobs and a savings policy. That's such a hard concept for this culture when we're inundated with consumer items and credit cards practically being thrown at us. What money does is create freedom for alternate choices."

After the debt is paid, either pay for everything with check or cash. If you do pay with a credit card then pay the entire balance each month.

Track Your Finances Every Month

Be aware of how you spend your money, including cash, check and credit card purchases. There are plenty of forms you can use to track your spending. Talk to an accountant or go to the library to look for forms or computer programs that will be the most useful to you. Keep a separate form for your sources of income. (Unfortunately, this is usually a much shorter list.) Determine when your major bills are due each year, like property taxes, insurance payments, etc., so you can budget for them.

Find A Trustworthy Financial Planner/Advisor

You'll need to do some homework to find a good person to advise you on investing your money. One way to find someone is to ask people you trust and respect — and who are reasonably affluent. The big issue here is trust. It means having a relationship with a person who, with the exception of a close friend or a sexual partner, will know the most intimate aspects of your life. I told my advisor she should have a couch in her office since she deals with so many other issues when she handles people's money. There are plenty of magazines, books and seminars available to help you decide what will work best for you. It's your responsibility to perform due diligence in finding someone with whom you can relate well.

Get In The "Right" Mind About Financial Responsibility And Independence

Having made your financial goals and taken action on them sets you on the right road to accomplishing what you want. The other part is thinking and believing you deserve to have everything you want. This takes a big leap of faith for some, but it doesn't cost you anything. What do you have to lose?

From *You Can't Afford the Luxury of a Negative Thought* by John-Roger and Peter McWilliams:

"If you persist in your thoughts of wealth, for example, this produces a consciousness of wealth — an overall state of being that is open, accepting, abundant and flowing — and this consciousness of wealth tends to produce the physical manifestations of wealth: houses, cars, cash and a special edition of *Lifestyles of the Rich and Famous.*

"'But,' someone once protested, 'I don't have any money and I worry about it all the time.' This person was proving the point, but in reverse. Worry is a form of fear, in this case a fear of poverty. This person, in holding an ongoing series of thoughts about poverty, created a consciousness of poverty, which created a lack of everything but bills, which caused more worry, which created more poverty.

"Positive thoughts yield positive results — loving, caring and sharing; health, wealth and happiness; prosperity, abundance and riches."

You should have a healthy attitude about why you're saving and investing. There is a difference between having enough for retirement and waiting until then to start enjoying life. You need to be

> "There are two things to aim at in life: first, to get what you want; and, after that, to enjoy it. Only the wisest of mankind achieve the second."
> – Logan Pearsall Smith

responsible and solvent while living and enjoying the present. (These aren't mutually exclusive concepts.) If you're having fun today and also saving for tomorrow, you're probably going to enjoy both.

Give your attitude the deathbed test: Picture yourself saying one of two things: "Boy, oh boy, I sure am glad I put off all those trips and my dream cottage on the lake in the mountains so I can leave all my money to my family?" Or "I have some great memories of my trips to wonderful places in the world and the times I was able to be with my family and friends at my mountain home. I'm glad I was able to provide them with as many wonderful memories as I have."

> "There are people who have money and people who are rich."
> – Coco Gabrielle Chanel

If all you're doing is gloating over your net worth on the balance sheet every month, you might want to rethink your life. If you're in abject poverty you, too, need to revisit your circumstances and come up with a plan to turn this around.

> "If money is your hope for independence, you will never have it. The only real security that a man can have in this world is a reserve of knowledge, experience and ability."
> – Henry Ford

My financial goals my seem a bit simplistic to a more sophisticated financier. However, they cover the basics and work well for me.

- I save X amount of money every month.
- I pay all my bills every month (or I have a plan to pay them all off).
- I track my income and expenditures every month.
- I will find a financial planner.

Affirmations:

I give myself permission to have a healthy financial balance sheet.

I deserve and have anything I really want.

I am alert to beneficial financial opportunities and I take action.

I do good and fun things with my money today, knowing that I have planned wisely and will be taken care of tomorrow.

7

Becoming Whole Through Friends And Family

Value: I love my family and friends.

In a half-assed world, you're too busy to cultivate your relationships with friends and family. Becoming whole means strengthening your relationships by nurturing those that are healthy and admitting that you need other people in your life — and that they need you, too.

We moved a lot when I was growing up. The good thing about living in different places is that I learned to change like a chameleon and get along with a wide variety of people. The sad part is that I've had no contact with any of the kids from grade school or junior high and only a couple of friends from high school, and all of my relatives live in other states. I feel a sense of loss and am somehow disconnected from my past because of this.

We are brought up to be self-reliant, rugged individualists. To be anything else means that we're weak and somehow lacking. (You can bet the Marlboro man never had a friend accompany him to the bathroom!) To need the help of a family member or friend has been viewed by many as nothing short of a genetic defect.

> "Independence? That's middle-class blasphemy. We are all dependent on one another, every soul of us on earth."
> – George Bernard Shaw

When I entered the world of work, the unspoken word was that somehow I was already supposed to know how to do everything. Asking for help was a surefire way to get derailed from the fast track. It took me a long time to realize how goofy (and debilitating) this notion is. I finally reprogrammed these subliminal messages and now realize that it's not only okay to need others and ask for their help, but our very lives depend on it.

In the *12 Steps to Self-Parenting,* Philip Oliver-Diaz and Patricia A. O'Gorman show that self-reliance is a byproduct of needing to have control — and what a sham this so-called control is:

> "In an attempt to control everyone and
> everything around us, we become obsessed
> with being totally self-reliant. We believe, in
> our drive to control, that our self-will can

make anything we want happen. We close
out people, refuse to help and deny our need
for the support and comfort for which our
inner-child cries. We learn to live in a desert.
We learn to live in isolation.

"We create a world in which we are all
we need to get by. We become compulsive
about being self-reliant to such a degree that
when we finally need to let others help us,
we can't or don't know how. And so
husbands, wives, lovers and friends leave us
because they feel useless and unnecessary.
And we remain alone in our totally
controlled, self-imposed prison, in solitary
confinement. And we forget that we have the
key to set ourselves free.

We've all heard that babies who aren't held and
cuddled can literally die of loneliness. A lot of adults, in the
midst of all the hubbub, are also dying of loneliness by
trying to live up to the image of the rugged individualist and
ultimately end up leading emotionless and empty lives.
Kids join gangs to fill the void left by broken families and
uninvolved communities. The gang becomes the family and
community for these youngsters. It's a lousy alternative, but
it's something. They're still dying, but at least it's not from
loneliness.

Remember how good you felt when you had the
privilege of helping someone out? Allow someone to help
you out, so he or she can experience those feelings, too.

Our Relationships With Friends And Family
Are Always Changing

All of us have families and all of us need friends. There's one school of thought that says you didn't choose your family but at least you can choose your friends. Another school of thought says that on the cosmic level you did choose your families for what they have to teach you, for better or worse, and you attract friends into your life for what they have to teach you, for better or worse.

> "When you love someone ... you do not love him or her in exactly the same way, from moment to moment. It is an impossibility. And yet this is exactly what most of us demand. We have so little faith in the ebb and flow of life, or love, or relationships. We leap at the flow of the tide and resist in terror its ebbs."
>
> – Anne Morrow Lindbergh

Whether you subscribe to the dumb-luck theory ("Bad joss getting into this rotten family.") or the I-chose-this-family-to-learn-some-sort-of-lesson theory, your relationships with friends and family are powerful. They serve as a way to understand yourself better. Shakti Gawain in *Living in the Light* expands on this thought:

"Relationships are not outside — they are inside of us; this is the simple truth that we must recognize and accept. My true relationship is my relationship with myself — all others are simply mirrors of it.... If I am committed to myself and the truth, I will attract others with equal commitment.

"Because many of us have never really

learned how to take care of ourselves, our relationships have been based on trying to get someone else to take care of us.

"... This system doesn't work very well. Other people are seldom able to fulfill our needs consistently or successfully, so we get disappointed and frustrated. Then we either try to change the other people to better suit our needs (which never works), or we resign ourselves to accepting less than we really want. Furthermore, when we're trying to give other people what they want, we almost invariably do things we don't really want to do and end up resenting them, either consciously or unconsciously."

Whew! This subject could (and does) fill volumes and has worn out a lot of leather on therapists' couches. The purpose of this chapter is not to dissect and heal relationships but to provide thoughts on the value of having people in our lives and how to nurture those relationships we choose to nurture.

There are some relationships that aren't worth nurturing. You know which those are. They're the ones that don't make you feel very good about yourself. It's the relationship with the "friend" who is critical and judgmental. It's the relationship with the spouse who only values you for the amount of money you make. It's the relationship with the person who

> "Keep away from people who try to belittle your ambitions. Small people always do that, but the really great make you feel that you, too, can somehow become great."
> – Mark Twain

puts down your ideas and makes you lose confidence. It's the physically and emotionally abusive relationship that is not only demeaning but dangerous.

Over a lifetime we outgrow a lot of our relationships with family and friends. In my drinking and smoking days, I loved meeting friends at a bar to — what else — drink and smoke! Now, I prefer to take a walk with a friend or meet somewhere for coffee or have a leisurely dinner. That doesn't make me better than my friends back at the bar; it just means I've decided to make changes in my life that I think will help me live longer and healthier. It's okay to grow in new directions and move on. It's not okay to expect others to grow at the same rate or move in the same direction as you do, when you do — if they ever do.

Make the choice to be around upbeat people with a positive attitude toward life. Anyone can sit around and bemoan the state of the world, the fact that her marriage isn't working out, her job stinks or, despite workouts, her body continues to travel south. You should be with those who see the glass half full and who are working to improve their lives rather than sitting around complaining about them. That doesn't mean you can't talk about your problems, just try not to talk about the same one all the time.

We have a tendency to take those closest to us for granted. And those people are the very ones we'd

> True friendship is like sound health; the value of it is seldom known until it is lost.
>
> – Charles Caleb Colton

call on if we had an emergency in the middle of the night! Minding these relationships doesn't have to take a lot of time, money or energy. All it takes is a little bit of planning and thought.

Following are some ideas on how you can "grow" your relationships:

Family

- Make a list of birthdays, anniversaries and other significant events and write them on your calendar at the beginning of each new year. At the beginning of each month get the cards, gifts, etc. to be given/mailed at the appropriate times.
- Consider writing a family newsletter. A large "yours, mine and ours" family across the street does this with their scattered family. The kids have even made it into a moneymaking project by selling subscriptions. It is a way for them to stay in touch, while the "reporters" gather information to write. Everyone looks forward to their quarterly family updates.
- Keep in touch with relatives with a note or calls. If you live in the same town, and it's not a long distance call, do it more often.
- If you live close to older relatives, ask them to your house for dinner or take them out. Do this with young ones in college or just starting out.

Add your own, unique ideas to the list.

Friends

- Make a list of birthdays, anniversaries and other significant events at the beginning of each year and mark them on your yearly calendar. At the beginning of each month get the cards, gifts, etc. to be given/mailed at the appropriate times.
- Keep in touch. Buy a tablet of cheap note paper and write a note each month to a friend who lives out of town. If you have a computer, type up a quick note just to let him know you're thinking about him. If you're on the Net, send him E-mail.
- For no reason do something thoughtful for a friend.
- Schedule quarterly getaways with friends.
- Schedule quarterly potlucks with friends.
- Make a list of friends, local and out-of-town, with whom you want to talk each month. Call the out-of-towners during the cheap calling times.
- Be a pal to one of your friend's kids. Take him or her to the zoo or a movie, a concert, a hike or to lunch or dinner.

Add your own, unique ideas to the list.

Significant Other

- Write down his/her birthday and other important dates. (Don't laugh. I thought my husband's birthday was the day before it was, and he totally forgot our 12th wedding anniversary!)
- Do all the planning for a night out or a weekend away (including arranging for child and pet care).
- Do something unexpected:
  Take her a cup of coffee.
  Wash his car.
  Pay for dinner out.
  Offer to do the grocery shopping.
  Buy the book she's been talking about — or check it out from the library.
- Spend a day doing anything (legal, not harmful or too disgusting to you) he or she wants to do.
- Let him have the television remote control for an entire weekend (if it's not already permanently grafted to his hand).
- Make a coupon book with things like: Redeem for back rub, breakfast in bed, sex under the dining room table, I'll take the kids away and you can have the afternoon to yourself, etc.
- Write letters for significant occasions.

Add your own, unique ideas to the list.

Do the same for your children (I consider my child my other significant other). They deserve some special treatment, too. Make a coupon book for back rubs, breakfast in bed, I'll play games with you for two straight hours without answering the phone, a visit to the museum. (One of my fondest memories is something that my dad started with me. He wrote a note each night, which he placed on my pillow. I wrote back and left mine on his pillow. We called them the Tiny Tots Notes. I've started doing the same with my son. Nothing preachy — just an "I love you" and "I'm proud of who you are." (This works for your partner, too.) Take your child out on a date a couple times a year — just the two of you.

The effort that you put into your relationships will come back in spades. But don't do it expecting to get anything. Do it because you want to. That way, if anything good does come out of it, it will be an added bonus. Put another way, in *The Last Self-Help Book Before Getting Results,* Jerome Lund writes:

"If we want love, we begin by giving love, first to ourselves and then to others, and finally to the world at large. If we will do that, we will find ourselves with more friends than we know what to do with. We will find our present relationships improving immeasurably, and if we want romantic love or a lifetime partner, we shall have that also."

Understand that the nature of all relationships changes over time. Nothing remains static. You and your best college buddy may have

"Make new friends but keep the old; some are silver and the other gold."
— Girl Scout camp song

nothing in common after 10 years away from the dorm. You and your significant other may change courses. You and your mother may reverse roles as caretaker. You and your own child's relationship should change as he or she matures (and as you mature, for that matter). Go with the flow of the relationships. Let those you love know it — all the time — even if it does make them suspicious.

Following are stories from the perspectives of a man and a woman whose family life gave them the values of solid relationships:

Gary, a Teddy bear of a man, is a professor. Married for 35 years, he and his wife have known each other since the first grade. Family and friends are extremely important to both of them.

"The male members in my family are very close. There are seven kids in my family, five of us are boys, and we all like each other. My wife is one of six and for the most part, all of her siblings are acquainted with and like all of my siblings. We genuinely like each other and do things with each other. It makes me feel very fortunate, and I don't take it for granted. I feel like I've been blessed. I don't mean to sound corny, but it's true. I have a friend who hates his brother and doesn't like his mom and dad. He almost started crying because he's so envious of my relationship with my family. His reaction just underscored what I have. I also have friends who would go to the wall for me. All my life I've been blessed with wonderful friends. I took a long hike one day with a psychologist, and he was absolutely fascinated about how atypical my family is in certain ways. We're not carbon copies of each other, but we don't let the differences get in the way. The bonding with my brothers is

nurtured by annual backpacks, lots of phone calls, and a couple of major events every year that bring us together."

Doreen's slight build belies her great inner strength. People try to take a lot from her, and she lets them — to a point. In her 30s, she "did it her way" and survived a usually-fatal form of cancer, shunning her doctor's advice for amputation and chemotherapy.

"I have a unique perspective on family because I'm a twin. I've never been alone. I come from a large family with five sisters and brothers. We lived in rural South Dakota, and the nearest town was 35 miles away. So we learned the value of family, because members of my family became my friends. We were all we had! I've carried that with me all my life. There's an old saying that our greatest strength comes not from our pain but from our joy, and I've always felt a lot of joy from my friends and family. They are truly where my strength comes from. I nurture them through kindness, attentiveness, sharing and most of all, listening. Everybody needs attention. I feel that everybody needs strokes and hugs. We need a core group of friends. We can't spread ourselves too thin because our friends need quality from us."

I think it's worthwhile to create goals pertaining to family and friends that will help strengthen my relationships.

Goals:
- I remember my family and friends on birthdays and other special occasions.

- I call or write my immediate family twice a month.
- I keep in touch with in-town friends via phone and regularly call or write out-of-town friends.
- I address and try to resolve conflicts or misunderstandings as soon as they occur.

Affirmation: I love, respect and nurture my relationships with my friends and family.

8

Becoming Whole through Giving Back

Value: I give back to the world.

In a half-assed world, you only think about what's in it for you. To become whole, you reorient your thinking to include what you can do for others.

Look at the face and posture of a child who's just done a good deed for someone.

You've heard the expression, "Give 'til it hurts." That is not what's meant by giving back to the world. The title of this chapter could have had the word "charity" in it. But that's not what I mean, either. Charity sounds like you're coming out of your ivory tower to bestow favors and trinkets on those lucky enough to breathe the same air as you. By giving, I mean taking the time to become involved with, and help, others. This can equate to time or money or both.

A lot of giving is good. A little giving is good. No giving is not good. Helping others makes us feel magnanimous and is a good example to set for our family, children and friends. Helping others is good for the world.

What stops a lot of people from becoming involved outside of work and the daily grind is a feeling that becoming involved means spending many hours a week, which most of us don't have.

It doesn't have to be that way at all. When you're in a position to give a few hours a week, do it. If it's only a couple of hours a

"To serve is beautiful, but only if it's done with joy and a whole heart and a free mind."
— Pearl S. Buck

month, do it. I used to put in a lot of hours at a women's safehouse. Then I tutored kids in reading at my son's school once a week for a couple of hours. Your giving does not need to become a lifelong commitment to a single cause. In my case, the cause has changed to mesh with the rest of my life. So can yours.

Popular author Anthony Robbins made the point that while the problems that plague the world seem overwhelming, it's through the efforts of the individuals that change is ultimately made. I call this the "brick by brick" process. The more we as

"Human service is the highest form of self-interest for the person who serves."
— Elbert Hubbard

individuals can do on a volunteer basis, the less the government has to do on a tax and spend basis.

You may not be able to devise a better distribution system to end world hunger (maybe you can), but you can make a difference in a kid's life by helping him learn to read. He may not remember you, but you'll surely remember helping him.

There is no dearth of people and causes from which to choose. If something doesn't occur to you right off hand, following is a list of ideas to get you thinking:

- Go to the school nearest you and ask what kind of help it needs.
- Call your local United Way or its equivalent.
- Volunteer at the church of your choice.
- Consider the Dumb Friend's League.
- Help out once a year with a fund-raiser.
- Help with the Special Olympics in your area.
- Visit senior citizens at a nursing home.
- Become a Big Brother or Big Sister.
- Select an individual or family to mentor.
- Become involved in local or national politics.

Follow your interests and use your talents, and you'll find someone or something to give back to.

It's absolutely true that one of the great secrets of the world is that by serving others you serve yourself. As Emerson said, "It is one of the beautiful compensations of this life that no one can sincerely try to help another without helping himself."

Joy comes back from giving.

Don't wait to give back to the world until 1) you get the promotion at work (you'll have even less

> "The pleasure we derive from doing favors is partly in the feeling it gives us that we are not altogether worthless."
>
> – Eric Hoffer

time then); 2) the kids are grown (it would be nice of you to set the example so your kids know that giving and service should be a part of their lives in their lifetimes); 3) you straighten out all your drawers, organize your closets and clean your garage (oh, come on!); 4) you're making X amount of money a year (when you get there, you'll just need more).

Start now. You're never too young, too old nor too busy to put yourself out there to give back to the world.

Following are stories that show how beneficial volunteering is, and though the effort is unselfish, doing for others always has a big payback for the giver:

⚜

Sarah, 48, works full-time raising two children and makes sure that she and her family give something back to their community. It's become a natural part of all of their lives.

"I grew up in a family that did no volunteer work. I think my dad made financial contributions to political parties, but I never saw anyone do volunteer work in the sense that they physically went somewhere to help someone out. I always sensed that this was not the way to live. But for a long time I just didn't make the time to do anything for anybody else either. I guess that is the 'Charity begins at home' mentality. Once I had children, I wanted them to know that someone else wasn't going to solve all of the ills of society. I wanted them to know that we have to do our part, however small, to help others. I'm trying to set an example so it becomes a part of their lives — not something they pick up much later in life, as I did."

As the president of his own company and father of five, George didn't have much left to give. Now that he's a healthy, vibrant, 76-year-old retiree, he's making up for lost time.

"I've worked all my life and raised five children. After I retired I played for awhile. A couple years later I figured I'd better do something more with my life. That's when I got involved with the school system. I've got the time and the background to contribute by helping sort out some of their problems. Besides, my grandchildren are going to be going to these schools pretty quick. I'd like to think they're going to get everything they deserve from the system."

Jere's one of the first people others think to call when there's a project that needs to get done. The adage of calling on the busiest person you know is true of her. She's been a high achiever all her life, so it's no surprise that Jere had placed volunteering high on her list of priorities.

> "You have not done enough, you have never done enough, so long as it is still possible that you have something to contribute."
> – Dag Hammarskjold

"When my sister was diagnosed with multiple sclerosis, my volunteer work helped me deal with the frustrations of not being able to do much for her. Volunteering has given me more compassion for others and their problems. Whenever I feel like I have problems, I only need to look around to see that others are worse off than I am. I've met some really generous and compassionate people. My dad had been involved in Lion's Club and my mom was an election judge so it's always been around. I was involved in school clubs in high school. And the company I worked

for had a corporate culture that supported volunteerism. The best result is personal satisfaction in that I'm not focusing on myself. I have skills I can use to help others and have been doing it long enough to know the ins and outs."

Again, It's important to establish in writing what you want to accomplish.

Goal:

• I will make a time and/or money commitment to help with a cause(s) I believe in.

Affirmation: I love to help others and know that by giving back to the world I benefit as much as those I'm helping.

9

Becoming Whole Through Learning

Value: I love to learn.

In a half-assed world, you think that once you've finished your formal schooling you're finished with learning. Not only that, but now you're supposed to be an expert. To become whole, you have to realize that life is about learning — not being an expert — and that the learning never stops. You will always be a student.

I hope I live to be a 150 years old. There is still so much for me to learn. I'm just now understanding relationships. I'm just now "getting" the messages in some of the Aesop's Fables I read as a child. I'm just now understanding what's really important to me. I want to go back to school and major in everything. I even want to try math again.

We're always learning. We learn from the work we do. We learn about human nature on our commute to work (you know the drill — who's flipping off who, who's darting in and out of traffic, who's singing and who's tweezing or shaving). Even when we're watching the evening news or taking a walk, we're learning. This is the peripheral learning that comes from living our day-to-day lives.

> "Our willingness to learn and to apply what we've learned — in a word, grow — is a hallmark of wealth."
> – John Rogers & Peter McWilliams

Another kind of learning is that which we elect to do. This learning is self-taught or in a classroom situation. It can be for credit, certification or just for the fun of it. It can be career-enhancing or for personal development. Learning can take on many forms.

Since my formal education ended, I've taken courses funded by my employer to enhance my professional skills. I've taken art classes (only my mother would think I'm good), quilting (a lifetime project), screen writing (and as a result wrote a yet-to-be-produced screenplay), meditation (still in progress) and exercise classes (will always be in progress). In addition, I've done extensive studying in the areas of personal growth and nutrition. My personal growth reading has led me on several different paths of study. As a result, I've used my reservoir of knowledge to write, to deal with customers and partners in my marketing business and to build relationships and better

> "The spiritual perfection of man consists in his becoming an intelligent being — one who knows all that he is capable of learning."
> – Maimonides

understand and appreciate my life. This chapter is to help you understand that learning can be among the more enriching parts of your life — if you choose to incorporate it into your Whole Life Plan.

Here are just a few ways in which you might want to start (or continue):

- Join or organize a book club — fiction or nonfiction — around a subject that interests you. If you don't know enough people, post a notice at the local library or bookstore. Bookstores are delighted to help with reading lists for book clubs.
- Check your cable channels. Some offer degree programs via cable, which, even if you don't want the degree, you can tune in and get the benefit of the lectures.
- Check your local museum for lectures or seminars of interest to you.
- If you didn't finish high school or college, get your GED or degree.
- If you're analytical, take a creative writing or art course.
- If you're creative, take time management course.
- Take a first aid course that includes CPR.
- Turn the tables around and teach your skill to others. By teaching, you learn your subject even better.
- If you're more adventurous, learn to roller-blade, hang-glide or surf.
- Learn more about your family history. Interview relatives. Find out how people in your family have dealt with births, deaths,

good times and bad times. Do they pull together to help each other out? Do they value maintaining contact even if they are miles apart? You'll discover a lot about yourself from this type of research. If you're lucky, you'll unearth some colorful or unsavory characters whose pasts have been kept a family secret for generations.

• Learn a new language — or two or three.

> "I grow old, ever-learning many things."
>
> — Solon

You can either learn a totally new subject or improve something at which you're already good. If you're particularly good at accounting, take an advanced course or get some updated software to further develop your accounting skills. If you've always wanted to learn car maintenance or remedial plumbing, get a book or have someone teach you.

I have a friend who recently changed all the bathroom faucets by herself. The way she went on you'd think she'd discovered the cure for PMS. Learning some "guy" skill was heady stuff for her, just as it is for some of my "guy" friends who have become proficient at cooking — even if it is just one specialty dish.

Another, and probably the most powerful avenue of learning, is being open to all the potential teachers that surround you. There is a Zen proverb that states, "When the student is ready, the teacher will appear." You'll find when you decide you're ready to learn something, by some coincidence, an opportunity (or the teacher) will present itself. A few months ago a friend was thinking it would be fun to learn Tai Chi. The next time she went to Blockbuster Video, she found a beginning Tai Chi tape on sale. A friend told me he wanted to learn something about foot reflexology. He didn't have a clue where to look or who to call. As chance (sure) would have it, he received a flyer in the mail a week later from someone offering a special on foot massages.

The message is to stay open to all avenues of learning. No one is expected to know it all. Plus, you'd be really obnoxious to be around if you did.

The first-person stories about learning that follow prove that you're never too old to learn new things, and that you benefit by enlarging your scope of understanding the world and your place in it:

⚜

Listening to Jackie, 43, one gets the impression that she's far older than her years. She's simply too wise to be in her early 40s. She is trying a lot of new and different things in her life right now, keeping what she likes and tossing out what she doesn't.

"As a child in the formal school setting, I did not do well. It wasn't interesting and it wasn't life. The kinds of classes I'm taking now deal with life and are life enhancing. They've given me a different space to learn from. Going to college and high school is learning, but the learning I'm doing now is soul learning. I think my learning now is going to benefit mankind. There's a common bond with every living thing on earth. The other way isn't working. We have to go within to help ourselves now. We have all the answers inside of us. Before, my learning was mental work … now it's my soul work. I'm learning from the feeling part and then the brain kicks in."

Bill is who we all want to be like when we're 70 — mentally sharp, physically fit and with a wry sense of humor to boot! When he's not playing golf and spit polishing a vintage car, Bill and his wife travel and visit numerous grandchildren scattered around the country.

"Up until the time I retired, I'd been in banking. The last ten years I was president of a bank. We retired and moved up to the mountains. I got a little bored living up in the mountains and I didn't really have a purpose and felt I was beginning to stagnate, so decided I wanted to go to law school. It was something I'd always wanted to do and now I had the time. I was definitely the oldest in my class. It was a far harder than I thought it would be. I have two sons who are attorneys, and they didn't think I'd make it. That was my incentive to hang tough. I thought that with all my experience I'd zip right in and ace it. I was dead wrong about that! Law school kept my mind going all the time, and even now I read everything I can get my hands on. I keep up with everything and read more now. I wish I'd been younger when I'd done it ... but what an accomplishment!"

Walk into Helen's house and you know she's on a lifetime learning quest. Books are everywhere. And what an eclectic assortment there is! She allows herself only so many bookshelves, so she is always donating piles of overflow, used books to the various book fairs around town.

> "The love of learning, the sequestered nooks, and all the sweet serenity of books."
> – Longfellow

"I have a favorite book store I like to go to. It's small and I've come to know the owners. I'm always open-minded

when I go in because I want them to give me their recom-
mendations on a good book to read. By having no precon-
ceived notions, I always learn something and read a book
that I would have had no reason to otherwise. Because of
this experience, I now ask a lot of people for their recom-
mendations on various things. I'm never disappointed and I
always learn something new."

    I try to learn or do something new each year.
Following are my learning goals for the next year or so:
- I will take a water colors class.
- I will take conversational Spanish
- I will take an Indian cooking class.

Affirmation: My life is enriched
by all that I can learn.

10

Becoming Whole Through Loving Life

Value: I love life.

In a half-assed world, you critically dissect the past and live in dread of what the future might bring. To become whole, you must live in the present and appreciate who you are, what you are and what you have at this very moment.

❧

A friend of mine told me that she hated every single part of her body when she was in high school. Now she looks back at her pictures and would give anything to look like that again.

❧

Loving life is an attitude. It's not being hysterically happy all the time. Nor is it ignoring or discounting all the evil and unhappiness in the world. Loving life is acknowledging that the only perfection is imperfection and accepting that as a truth. This is particularly heartening to those of us with our share of blemishes.

Loving life is the outlook you have toward your personal universe and how you deal with both the good and the bad things that happen. You can look at events in your life as problems to overcome or as opportunities for growth.

Hang Out With Other Life Lovers

Who do you turn to when you're feeling down? A life lover or a life hater? Someone who will make you feel better — or worse? Those are pretty easy questions to answer.

It's easy to spot a person who loves life. He or she is the person you want to be around. Just being in the same room or talking to a life lover makes you feel better. The lovers of life talk about themselves and what's going on, but more importantly, they really want to know about you and how you're doing. You can hear the energy in their voices and in way they carry themselves. They make you feel good about yourself.

Avoid life haters. You know them. They're the ones who, when asked how they're doing, will tell you in excruciating detail everything that's going wrong; their bad health (organ by organ), investments that have gone bust (and what lousy advice they got), friends who have betrayed them (and how this happens to them all the time), relationships that aren't working out (and how this happens to them all the time) and jobs in which they're stuck (but there's nothing better out there).

We all need to be able to discuss our problems. Friendship is all about being around to listen to your friends and for them to listen to us. But if all you hear are complaints, and the complaints always remain the same, you'd better figure out why you've made the choice to be around this type of person. Oh, yes. Life haters will swear to you that they love life, too. They're just being realistic. Spare me. These are truly half-assed people.

As a life lover, you appreciate yourself and your present circumstances right now. This doesn't mean that you have to be happy about the speeding ticket you got or the cancer diagnosis your doctor just gave you. You can choose to accept the diagnosis as a death sentence or look at it as a challenge. It can be a wake-up call to tell you that with whatever time you do have left, you'd damned sure better make the most of it. Shouldn't everyone act like they've just been given a cancer diagnosis, and live accordingly?

> "I am in the present. I cannot know what tomorrow will bring forth. I can know only what the truth is for me today."
> — Igor Stravinsky

> "Don't become so obsessed with the goal that the process is not enjoyable. Send the light of your own loving ahead of you. When you get there, the loving will have prepared a place for you. Be kind, gentle and enjoy the journey."
> — John Rogers & Peter McWilliams

Try this experiment: For one whole week, make an effort to live in the present and appreciate your surroundings, the people who enter your life, the food you eat and the work you do. Make 25 yellow Post-it notes that say, "There is only now." Stick them on your mirrors, your doors, your appliances, your pictures, your TV, your car dashboard, every fifth square of toilet paper, your pillow and favorite chair. These notes will be the trigger to keep you focused on now — not what was or what will be. For most, this will be much more difficult than it sounds. It is an effort to stay in the moment.

Living in the present doesn't mean that you can't plan for tomorrow. "There is only now" counts when you're making reservations for your trip to Disney World in six months. You can enjoy the anticipation of the trip and enjoy planning it today.

"There is only now" doesn't, however, mean withdrawing your life savings and squandering it. It's a reminder not to hoard all the money for your retirement. If you get run over by a truck tomorrow, the only good all that money is going to do is buy you a great funeral.

There are a lot of things you can do to stay grounded in the present to build the awareness of what you have here and now:

Start Each Day By Mapping It Out In Your Mind

When you wake up, remember what you have to do for the day. Visualize the things you need to do and see them all going the way you want them to. Visualize yourself accomplishing your tasks easily, happily and in a relaxed frame of mind. At the end of the day, quickly review the events and then release them. They're over. If you have any problems you're working on, ask the question of yourself before you go to sleep. You'd be surprised how many answers you can find in your dreams — if you're open to them.

Make Positive Contacts With The People You Meet

On your way to work, treat people on the road the way you want to be treated. Let people merge into your lane. When people allow you to merge, wave your thanks. (Make that a wave, not a mid-digital salute!) When you get your morning coffee, over-tip the waitress or waiter. Always smile and say thanks. If you have to stand in line at the bank, dry cleaners or grocery store, make good use of that time and either do some deep breathing or chit chat with someone else in line. When you deal with work colleagues, your child's teacher, your stockbroker, etc., remember they're human and have problems, too. Walk the proverbial mile in their shoes so you can see things from their perspectives. Put yourself out there in terms of helpfulness, smiles and friendliness. What you give, you'll get back.

Pamper Yourself

There is nothing selfish about taking care of yourself and taking time to make yourself feel and look better.

The following suggestions can cost a lot or nothing. You can decide what you want to spend the money on and what you'd rather do yourself.

> "There are some days when I think I'm going to die from an overdose of satisfaction."
>
> – Salvador Dali

- Take candlelight bubble baths. Play soothing music. Read a book or meditate. This is one of my favorite freebies. I try to do it once a week. I lock the door and tell everybody to leave me alone.

- Have a massage once a month (once a week or every day, if you can afford it). This is a wonderful way to relax and really be in the present with someone who can work the kinks of the day out. If you can't afford it, find a friend with whom you can trade massages. Rub your own feet. (This is the worst case scenario, kind of like cooking for yourself. Why bother?) Or trade out a foot rub. This is an easy one you can even teach your children to do.

- Have a facial or spend an entire day at a local spa. Or give yourself a weekly facial. Set aside the time for this. Don't put on a facial mask and then run around the house doing the laundry or vacuuming. Relax, read, listen to music.

- Give yourself a manicure or pedicure.

- If you belong to a club, after every workout, take time for the whirlpool and/or steam room. This is an excellent reward and a nice place to meditate for awhile.

- Take an hour and listen to a book or motivational tape while you just sit or needlepoint.

- At least once a month go to dinner with friends. Pick a wonderful restaurant, have wine (or imported mineral water) and take a few hours to enjoy the time together. If you can't pull this off financially, do it at home using your best or favorite plates, candles and linens. Make it an event. Make it a ritual.

- Go on weekend retreats by yourself, with a friend or with your partner. I do this a few times a year and always come back home relaxed, refreshed and revitalized. The change of scenery by being out of town helps put things into perspective. I recognize that going off somewhere and leaving family behind is terribly disconcerting to a lot of people. It has, surprisingly, raised the eyebrows of people I've met when I've gone away. If you can feel comfortable and not guilty about making occasional getaways, then do it.

• Make a refuge or "nest" — a space in your home where you can escape. For me, it's my office. But it can be just a corner of a room, your bathtub, the back porch, your bed. Make this the special place to go when you need time to yourself. Let others know that when you're in your "nest" you're fluffing your feathers and no one is to disturb you. Allow others in your family to make their nests, too. And respect their feather-fluffing time.

• Several times a day, stop and notice your surroundings. This sounds so simplistic, but it will make you stop thinking ahead and appreciate what's in front of you right now.

• Take a walk at noon or after dinner, not for aerobic exercise but to really look at the fall leaves on the ground, the winter snow on the tree branches, the spring flowers or the summer grasses.

• Study a flower. Sketch it. Even a dandelion growing between the cracks in the concrete is pretty remarkable if you'll take the time to look at it! If you can't get outdoors, look out the window or at the dust bunnies under your bed.

- Lie on the grass and find pictures in the clouds.
- Stop yourself and take three deep breaths and just appreciate the moment.
- Think about a happy moment from your past and feel that way now. Tell yourself this is the way you feel most of the time.
- Go someplace you usually go and really look at it. It may just be a room in your house or a corner of your backyard.

Add your own ways to pamper yourself.

> "If you spend all your time in a positive future, when will you appreciate the present? The present is the future you dreamed of long ago. Enjoy it."
> – John Rogers & Peter McWilliams

Keep A Journal

This is a great place to celebrate life events, vent your anger and disappointments, remember dreams and chronicle your life. It's wonderful to be able to go back and see how far you've come in your development. It's also a good barometer to see if you're stuck in a rut and need to get out.

Throughout my life I've kept journals. (Can anybody tell me when journal became a verb?) I've "journaled" inconsistently but enough to have really embarrassing parts of my life to look back on. There's a lot I didn't put down for fear of it getting in the wrong hands (something I have personal experience of, since as a little sister I got my hands on my older sister's diary and was able to quote entire passages at the dinner table). I wrote down my thoughts when I made a major move to a town in which I was a complete stranger. And I've written about my mid-life growth, especially about my pregnancy, the birth of my son and all the incumbent neuroses associated with that. I've included entries about my childhood and high school memories — sweet, naive, idealistic and at times (reading back) humiliating. Recorded memories do make you appreciate how far you've come — or haven't.

> "What a wonderful life I've had! I only wish I'd realized it sooner."
> – Colette

Journal-keeping can become a big asset in your life. Don't underate your thoughts. You don't have to be Eleanor Roosevelt or Churchill to keep a journal. So maybe you're not making world history — but you are making history of some sort — and who can say that you won't make big history? In today's mobile society, most of us don't grow up around our relatives. As a result, we've lost the art of handing down great stories in our families.

If I hadn't written it down, who in my family would remember that my maternal grandfather was too old to participate in World War II, so as a high school teacher he volunteered to scrape and paint battleships? It was while doing this volunteer work that he fell off some scaffolding and died. My paternal grandfather died of heart disease, as did his sons. This is important historical and health information to have.

Keeping a journal can have several benefits:
- If you're really working with a journal, you can work through emotional problems. I have a friend who writes down all of her dreams and therapy sessions and has been able to write herself out of a lot of emotional issues.
- If you have children, you can leave a piece of you to them, or to your family's designated historian. It's interesting history.
- If you record your personal progress, it can be a testament to your growth.

Journal-keeping doesn't have to be a big deal. Keep a tablet by your bed and write whenever the mood strikes. If every night suits you, do it. If a couple times a month is all you can manage, do it. If once a year is all you can muster, do that. The main thing is to write something down that you'll have to look back on next week, next year, next millennium.

My journal writing has increased immensely now that I have a laptop computer. I take it with me on trips so I can write anywhere, anytime. It's also the only file I have password protected so I know no one will be able to see it until I'm ready. I'm amazed at the intensity with which I wrote about topics several years ago, which deserve just a yawn today. It's wonderful to see where I was and where I am now. It's also not-so-wonderful to see where I was and and some of the ruts I'm still in.

> "Prayer is good, but while calling on the gods, a man himself should lend a hand."
> – Hippocrates

If you don't have a clue where to start, buy *The Diary*

of Ann Frank or *A Woman of Independent Means* or Benjamin Franklin's or Ann Morrow Lindberg's autobiographies. The writings of these people can either inspire you or intimidate you. Choose the former so you'll do your own. Remember: it doesn't have to be perfect!

Read, Listen To Music And Limit Television

Read inspirational books, listen to your favorite music and cut your television viewing in half (at least). As you surround yourself with positive, life-loving people, you can do the same with the books you read, the music you listen to and the television programming you choose to view. The bibliography at the end of this book provides a list of my favorite books. Go to a book store or library and ask for help. Check out classical music (or something you like) at the library. Every week, select just a few shows on television you're going to watch. Use the time you're not watching to write a letter, make a journal entry, take a walk, read to your child, meditate. You get the picture.

Laugh Until It Hurts

We take ourselves far too seriously. Lightening up should include a huge dose of laughter every day. If you're around dour, humorless people, get a new set of friends.

When I was with the telephone company, I worked with an incredible group of hardworking, professional, fun and laughter-loving people. I honest-to-God loved to get up and go to work most every day. We worked hard, but we took time to joke and laugh. In fact,

> "Laughter is by definition healthy."
> -- Doris Lessing

some of us had such a grand time, we sounded like we were having *too* much fun! The staid corporate culture had a hard time with this (Are the troops supposed to be enjoying themselves this much?), and in time those of us who were having *too* much fun were physically separated. This is truly a sad commentary on most work environments.

> "The most wasted day of all is that in which we have not laughed."
> – Nicolas Chamfort

Walk through any major business today and listen. Chances are you won't be bowled over by belly laughs and guffaws.

Someone once said, if you think you'll laugh about the situation tomorrow, why not laugh about it now? I sometimes stop myself short and crack up in the middle of nagging my son about something he's done or forgotten to do when I realize that I'm taking the infraction far too seriously. He'll look at me and start laughing, too. Catch yourself being too serious and have a laugh instead.

⚜

Here are two women who know the value of loving life:

Jean's a beautiful, self-contained woman. An avid reader, she recently decided to give water color classes a shot. Jean lost her husband several years ago, but has settled into a life which appears to be a happy one for her.

"My time is NOW! I've always lived my life with that philosophy. It's impossible to retrieve a moment from the past, so it's important that my mind and body work together to control what I choose to do with the next moment of my life. My husband lived that way, too. He went with his gut feelings in business and refused to agonize over decisions.

My mom, too. She always made decisions about what was going on at the present time. If it was a bad decision, she'd admit it and just go on. I refuse to dwell for weeks about something that may have gone wrong. I refuse to waste a moment of my life."

"Children enjoy the present because they have neither a past nor a future."
– Jean de la Bruyere

If it's true that the eyes are the windows to the soul, Sharalynn has quite a soul! She's a diminutive woman, and you get the sense that whatever she has to say, she's thought about it — and probably lived it, too.

"For a large part of my life, my past ran my present. When I discovered that, I was appalled because what was running my now *were the things I didn't like from the past — like hate, pain, sorrow, dread ... all of the negatives. I tried everything I knew to step beyond them, but they had a firm grip on my present. They colored and imbued everything I did. I started out in the corporate world and by 1974, I had achieved all of my goals. But I woke up one morning and said, 'If I'm where I wanted to be, why am I so miserable? Why do I feel hollow?' I didn't like what I'd become in order to be successful.*

"I'd been raised to achieve and have been labeled a high achiever always wanting to get more. But the question, in my mind was, 'more what?' That led me to take an inventory of my life, including family, marriage and profession. Everything began to shift at that point. My marriage ended because I wasn't receiving what I wanted. I had money, prestige, a wonderful home, but I wasn't receiving the emotional nurturing and care.

"I moved to the Virgin Islands for two years. Over those years, I joined groups, did individual counseling — both spiritual and psychological. I lived in the moment for what I wanted, rather than what others wanted. I explored what gave me pleasure and what gave me pain, and why. Now, I'm constantly asking myself what my intentions are here, what my true desires are and if I am being of service? I've committed my life to that. If one is in the flow of God, doorways open. What I finally figured out is as long as our past rules the now, our future is predestined. We are doomed to have the repetition of that which has already been. When we're firmly in touch with the now, we can seize the day and let our life guide us in the miracle of what life is.

"Promise Yourself ..."

To be so strong that nothing can disturb your peace of mind.

To talk health, happiness and prosperity to every person you meet.

To make all your friends feel that there is something good in them.

To look at the sunny side of everything and make your optimism come true.

To think only of the best, to work only for the best and expect only the best.

To be just as enthusiastic about the success of others as you are about your own.

To forget the mistakes of the past and press on to greater achievements in the future.

To wear a cheerful countenance at all times and give every living creature you meet a smile.

To give so much time to the improvement of yourself that you have no time to criticize others.

To be too large for worry, too noble for anger, too strong for fear and too happy to permit the presence of trouble."

– Imprinted on a business card I found

I've listed, as my final observation, some goals I've established to help me keep loving life. Maybe they can be a guide for you:

- I consciously set out to have only positive contacts with people.
- I regularly pamper myself.
- I have a "nest" or retreat.
- I take time to appreciate where I am and what I'm doing.
- I keep a journal.
- I read, listen to music and watch a minimum of television.

Affirmation: I love and appreciate all that I have in my life right now.

Afterword

So now what?

You've read the book. You realize that: a) you're so totally out of balance that if you were in a boat race you'd only go in circles, b) you're halfway there, but you're still listing like the leaning tower of Pisa or, c) you're satisfied with the way things are going right now (please write to me).

You can choose to: a) ignore everything and continue business as usual, b) try a couple of things and if they cut into your television time too much, drop them and reassume your position in the recliner or La-Z-Boy, or, c) give yourself the chance to make positive changes in your life, even if it's just one change every couple of years.

Don't make yourself crazy about becoming whole. It's not a job and nobody's keeping score. It's a lifestyle. Have fun with it. Celebrate your accomplishments and don't be hard on yourself. We all need "down time."

The kind of life you have is largely a reflection of your attitude and how you consciously set your course. We are all capable of great and

"Have the courage to live. Anyone can die."
– Robert Cody

wonderful things. We also are capable of doing nothing much with our lives. Becoming whole and having a balanced life is a journey full of highs and lows, detours, backtracking, getting totally lost and finding the way again. You can view your journey as an interminable hike you have to submit to until you die — or as a grand adventure.

Half-assed or whole? The choice is yours.

"Our deepest fear is not that we are inadequate. Our deepest fear is that we are powerful beyond measure.

"It is our light, not our darkness that frightens us. We ask ourselves, 'Who am I to be brilliant, gorgeous, talented and fabulous?'

"Actually, who are you not to be? You are a child of God. Your playing small doesn't serve the world.

"There's nothing enlightened about shrinking so that other people won't feel insecure around you.

"We were born to make manifest the glory of God that is within us. It's not just in some of us, it is in everyone.

"And as we let our own light shine, we unconsciously give other people the permission to do the same.

"As we are liberated from our fear, our presence automatically liberates others."

– 1994 Inaugural Speech
– Nelson Mandela

Bibliography

Allen, James, *As a Man Thinketh,* Personal Dynamic Institute, Minneapolis, MN, 1989.

Allen, Marc, *The Perfect Life,* New World Library, San Rafael, CA., 1992.

Anthony, Robert, *Advanced Formula For Total Success,* Berkeley Books, New York, 1988.

Bennett, Robert F., *Gaining Control — Your Key to Freedom and Success,* Pocket Books, New York, NY, 1987.

Card, Emily, Ph.D., *The Ms. Money Book,* E. P. Dutton, New York, NY, 1990.

Carper, Jean, *Stop Aging Now!,* Harper Collins, New York, NY, 1995.

Carter, Al, *Lifetimer Delivers Success,* Carter-Grove Publishing Company, Fountain Valley, CA, 1991.

Covey, Stephen R., *The 7 Habits of Highly Effective People,* Simon & Schuster, New York, NY, 1989.

Crum, Thomas F., *The Magic of Conflict,* Simon & Schuster, New York, NY, 1987.

Dyer, Dr. Wayne W., *Real Magic,* Harper Collins, New York, NY, 1992.

Dyer, Dr. Wayne W., *You'll See It When You Believe It,* Avon Books, New York, NY, 1989.

Easwaran, Eknath, *Your Life Is Your Message,* Nilgiri Press, Tomales, CA, 1995

Gawain, Shakti, *Creative Visualization,* Bantam Books, New York, NY, 1985.

Gawain, Shakti, *Living in the Light,* Whatever Publishing, Inc., Mill Valley, CA 1986.

Goodman, Alan, *The Big Help Book,* Minstrel Paperback, New York, NY, 1994.

Hay, Louise L., *You Can Heal Your Life,* Hay House, Santa Monica, CA, 1987.

Hill, Napoleon, *Think and Grow Rich Action Pack,* Penguin Books, New York, NY, 1988.

Lund, Jerome, Ph.D., *The Last Self-Help Book Before Getting Results,* The Barclay Press, San Francisco, CA, 1983.

MacLaine, Shirley, *Going Within,* Bantam Books, New York, NY, 1989.

Mander, Jerry, *In the Absence of the Sacred,* Sierra Club Books, San Francisco, CA, 1991.

Mander, Jerry, *Four Arguments for the Elimination of Television,* Quill, New York, NY, 1978.

Mindell, Earl, *Vitamin Bible,* Warner Books, New York, NY, 1991.

Passwater, Richard A., Ph.D., *The New Supernutrition,* Pocket Books, New York, NY< 1991.

Peck, M. Scott, M.D., *The Road Less Traveled,* Simon and Schuster, New York, NY, 1978.

Popcorn, Faith, *The Popcorn Report,* Harper Business, New York, NY, 1992.

Robbins, Anthony, *Awaken the Giant Within,* Simon & Schuster, New York, NY, 1991.

Roman, Sanaya and Parker, Duane, *Creating Money, Keys To Abundance* H. J. Kramer Inc., Tiburon, CA, 1988.

Shinn, Florence Scovel, The Secret Door to Success, DeVorss & Company, Marina del Rey, CA, 1940.

Shinn, Florence Scovel, *The Power of the Spoken Word,* DeVorss & Company, Marina del Rey, CA, 1945.

Sinetar, Marsha, *Do What You Love, The Money Will Follow,* Dell Publishing, New York, NY, 1987.

Singh, Tara, *A Gift for All Mankind,* Ballantine Books, New York, NY, 1992.

Spalding, Baird T., *Life and Teaching of the Masters of the Far East,* Vol. I, V, DeVorss & Company, Marina del Rey, CA, 1924.

Williamson, Marianne, *A Return to Love,* Harper Perennial, New York, NY, 1993.

Zukav, Gary, *The Dancing Wu Li Masters,* Bantam Books, New York, NY, 1979.

For Further Information

Barbara Reasoner is available for speaking engagements. She also presents *Becoming Whole In A Half-Assed World* to corporations, businesses and women's organizations.

Send inquiries to:
Barbara Reasoner
P.O. Box 9134
Englewood, Colorado 80111-1227

or

Fax: 303-741-5553

To order additional copies of

Becoming Whole In A Half-Assed World

Please send _____ copies at $14.95 for each book, plus $3.50 shipping and handling for the first book, $2 for each additional book in the same order.

Enclosed is my check or money order of $_____
or [ ] Visa   [ ] MasterCard
#_____ Exp. Date ____/____
Signature _____

Name _____
Street Address _____
City _____
State _____ Zip _____
Phone _____

(Advise if recipient and shipping address are different from above.)

For credit card orders call:
1-800-895-7323

or

Return this order form to:

BookPartners

P.O. Box 922
Wilsonville, OR 97070